Fighting for Africa

The Pan-African Contributions of Ambassador Dudley J. Thompson and Bill Sutherland

Edited by
Robert Johnson, Jr.

UNIVERSITY PRESS OF AMERICA,® INC.
Lanham • Boulder • New York • Toronto • Plymouth, UK

Library of Congress Control Number: 2009931792
ISBN: 978-0-7618-4791-5 (paperback : alk. paper)
eISBN: 978-0-7618-4792-2

∞™ The paper used in this publication meets the minimum
requirements of American National Standard for Information
Sciences—Permanence of Paper for Printed Library Materials,
ANSI Z39.48-1992

Africa unite:

'Cause we're moving right out of Babylon,

And we're going to our Father's land, yea-ea.

How good and pleasant it would be before God and man, yea-eah!

To see the unification of our Africans, yeah!

As it's been said a'ready, let it be done, yeah!

We are the children of the Rastaman;

We are the children of the Iyaman.

Bob Marley
("Africa Unite" from Survival album)

Contents

Preface

Over the past fifteen years I have had the opportunity to interview two of the giants of Pan-Africanism: Ambassador Dudley Thompson and Bill Sutherland. I first met Ambassador Thompson at an event at the Caribbean Cultural Center in Roxbury, Massachusetts. He had been invited to give a talk about reparations in the African world. Because I had an academic interest in the subject, I attended, and that meeting opened my eyes to his illustrious career as a Pan-African attorney. Furthermore, the fact that he was speaking in the heart of Boston's black community, rather than at a university, revealed the true depth of his commitment to the African diasporic community. From that initial meeting in 1993, I have met with Ambassador Thompson and obtained his story through face-to-face and telephonic interviews.

I first met Bill Sutherland in Roxbury, Massachusetts when I was invited by Muriel and Otto Snowden (founders of Freedom House) to their home to hear Bill talk about his life in Ghana, West Africa. The fact that Muriel and Otto, two pillars of Boston's Black community, hosted the talk was enough to draw a sizable crowd from Boston's black leadership. To our surprise we learned that Bill was the brother of Muriel. As a young professor I pursued a series of interviews with Bill Sutherland and when he arrived in Dar Es Salaam, Tanzania, East Africa in 1972 I conducted an extensive interview with him, but unfortunately lost the tape. So, when I unexpectedly met him at the African Studies Conference in Nashville, Tennessee in 2000 I conducted the short interview that is contained in this book.

At last I have been able to organize these interviews during my sabbatical in Charlotte, North Carolina. I owe a great deal of gratitude to many friends in Charlotte who provided love and support for my work. In particular I acknowledge the generosity of Valerie Todd and the Todd family and Jason Palmer. Without their support this project could not have been completed.

Introduction

Pan-Africanism, an evolving concept of African unity and self-help, has been a part of the African consciousness for over three centuries. From the first day, when African men and women were taken from Africa into slavery, until the present, they have never forgotten their connection to the ancestral home. Despite the separation of time and inhumane conditions, significant proportions of the African population in the diaspora never ceased viewing themselves as a displaced people or recognizing their responsibility to the struggle to free Africa from slavery, colonialism, and neo-colonialism.

This book is a series of interviews with two leading Pan-African activists and thinkers of the past century, Dudley J. Thompson and Bill Sutherland. They are from two different parts of the world, Panama/Jamaica and Glen Ridge, New Jersey and in the proud traditions of earlier Pan-Africanists, developed a clear Pan-African consciousness and engaged in sustained work on behalf of Africa.

How do we put the contributions of these men into the historical context of Pan-Africanism? The answer to this question will lie, in part, upon how we define the concept. Tony Martin, the world's leading authority on Marcus Mosiah Garvey, defines Pan-Africanism " . . . as the attempts by African peoples to link up their struggles for their mutual benefit."[1] At the heart of this definition is the notion that, regardless of where African people are found in the world, they are children of Africa and therefore possess a profound responsibility to the continent and its offspring. This conceptual notion of unity and concerted action has been expressed in the literature of intellectuals as well as in the pop culture of the masses. The former expression was ably represented in the five congresses that began in 1900, and culminated in the 1945 gathering that involved the leading black thinkers of the era. Peter Tosh, on the other hand, one of the greatest pop artists of the twentieth century, defined the concept in a manner that was more understandable by the masses and all those others who would listen: "Don't care where you come from, as long as you're a blackman, you're an African. No mind your nationality you have got the identity of an African."[2] Pan-African consciousness is, therefore, the precursor to any meaningful involvement in a Pan-African social movement.

PAN-AFRICAN CONSCIOUSNESS

The late great African-American writer, James Baldwin, once wrote: "To be a Negro in this country and to be relatively conscious is to be in a rage almost all the time."[3] Central to this idea of consciousness is the notion of transformation, of moving from a limited understanding of one's position and condition in the world, to a broader and more fulfilling one. Once one undergoes this conversion bitterness sets in, but also a sense of commitment to help lead one's brothers and sisters to a clearer understanding of self and the importance of African unity.

Nineteenth-Century Efforts

Pan-African consciousness has a long history in the western world. In the nineteenth century when the African slave trade reached its pinnacle, so did Pan-African consciousness. In the beginning of the century, free Africans in America, such as Paul Cuffe, traveled to West Africa where they engaged in trade and established repatriated communities. For example, there is evidence that Paul Cuffe established in Sierra Leone at least two such communities, the Friendly Society of Sierra Leone and the Society of Sierra Leone in Africa.[4]

Cuffe's initial voyage to Sierra Leone, West Africa on January 2, 1811 signaled the highest form of Pan-African consciousness: repatriation. While throughout the history of Pan-African consciousness we encounter men and women who write about Africa in glowing terms, very few actually disconnected themselves from the western world and re-established themselves in the motherland. Cuffe was the first to accomplish such a feat and his actions revealed tremendous skills and commitment as he utilized his own resources to build and equip his ship, *The Traveller*. He was determined to give his people an opportunity to return to Africa, not only in a ship built by African-Americans, but also captained and crewed by the children of Africa. His crew of nine men, however, were all descendants of Africa, with the exception of Abraham Rodin, a Swedish apprentice, who in 1807 attached himself to Cuffe to learn: " . . . seamanship and other industry . . . "[5]

When he arrived in Sierra Leone at Bens Island on March 1, 1811, he was enthusiastically welcomed and three days later dined with the Governor of the Island, Captain Edward Henry Columbine. Soon thereafter, he visited local schools, sold some of his products, hired local Africans to assist him, and sat in on the trial of a Portuguese slaver. Unlike trials in America where African people had no rights, in Sierra Leone, he witnessed the slaver being found guilty of engaging in illegal slave trade and witnessed the proceeds of the ship being distributed to the slaves who had been set free.[6] This exploratory trip in 1811 set the stage for his greatest achievement in 1815, i.e. the repatriation of thirty-eight African-Americans. This concrete expression of Pan-African-ism represented the highest form of African consciousness. The repatriates, for the most part, came from good, solid families who pooled their resources to pay for the return home to Africa. But it was his consciousness of Africa as the homeland of Africans in the diaspora that set his repatriation goals in motion.

Other prominent and highly educated individuals in the nineteenth century possessed similar consciousness and repatriated to Africa as well. John Brown Russwurm, who was born in Jamaica in 1799, became one of the first individuals of African descent to graduate from an American college (Bowdoin College, 1826). Russwurm established the first African-American newspaper in the United States in 1827, *Freedom's Journal*, before uprooting himself for Africa in 1829. In Liberia he edited the *Liberia Herald*, worked as Superintendent of Education, and later served as Governor of Cape Palmas Colony for fifteen years until his death in 1851. Other highly educated individuals who embraced a Pan-African consciousness and organized expeditions to Africa to explore the possibility of repatriation were Robert Campbell and Martin Delany, both of whom explored the Niger Valley of Nigeria through their Niger Valley Exploration Mission.

The most important proponent of the Pan-African philosophy in the nineteenth century, however, was Edward Wilmot Blyden. Blyden was born in August, 1832 on St. Thomas and repatriated to Liberia in January 1851. As a journalist, professor, and political activist, he developed a philosophy of Pan-African consciousness that placed Africa and its people at the center of world history and culture. Through his writings he advanced an Afro-centric consciousness at a time when the western world's campaign to totally denigrate African people had reached its highest point. To counter the racist propaganda of the West, Blyden published several pamphlets: "Hope for Africa," "The Negro in Ancient History," and "Africa's Service to the World."[7] Through his major works, *Christianity, Islam and the Negro Race* and *African Life and Customs*, he established Africa's place in world history and the importance of African-centered educational and religious systems.

Other kinds of consciousness took on more radical forms. David Walker, another free man who lived in Boston, published his *Walker's Appeal* in 1829, which called upon Africans in America to understand their "wretched" condition and to resist slavery with violence, if necessary. Nat Turner of Virginia in 1831 actually resorted to violent revolutionary struggle in a failed attempt to free himself and his people from the tentacles of slavery.

PAN-AFRICAN MOVEMENTS

There has been much confusion among scholars on the question of when the Pan-African movement began. The most widely accepted position has been that it began with the Paris meeting of intellectuals convened by W.E.B. Du Bois in 1919. Others have argued, convincingly, that the Trinidadian lawyer Henry Sylvester Williams convened the first group of individuals in London in the year 1900. However, Professor Esedebe has assembled even more compelling evidence that the first social movement of Africanists for the unity and redemption of Africa occurred in Chicago, Illinois on August 14, 1893.

Chicago Congress on Africa of 1893

This one-week Congress was international in make up and drew some of the most prominent Afro-centric leaders of the period, such as Alexander Crummell and Bishop Henry McNeil Turner of the African-Methodist Episcopal Church (A.M.E.). The Congress also caught the attention of Edward Wilmot Blyden and Booker T. Washington, who both planned to give papers, but were unable to attend.[8]

African Association

On September 24, 1897, Henry Sylvester Williams and others launched the African Association in London, England. The Association adopted as one of its main purposes the establishment of a movement against European imperial aggression. The movement would:

" . . . encourage a feeling of unity; . . . facilitate friendly intercourse among Africans in general; . . . promote and protect the interests of all subjects claiming African descent wholly or in part, in British Colonies and other places especially in Africa, by circulating accurate information on all subjects affecting their rights and privileges as subjects of the British Empire, and by direct appeals to the Imperial and local Governments."[9]

Twentieth Century Efforts
Pan-African Congress of 1900

The organizing efforts of the African Association paid off in the holding of the first Pan-African Congress in Europe. Between July 23 and 25, 1900, thirty-two Africans and their supporters gathered in London, England and established the following objectives: First, to bring into closer touch with each other the peoples of African descent throughout the world. Second, to inaugurate plans to bring about more friendly relations between the Caucasian and African races; third, to start a movement looking forward to the securing to all African races living in civilized countries their full rights and to promote their business interests.[10]

A good cross-section of individuals from the African diaspora attended this conference. Particularly important was the substantial contingent of women from the United States, which included Anna J. Cooper of Washington, D.C. and Anna H. Jones of Missouri. W.E.B. Du Bois, also in attendance, would play a key role in subsequent conferences.

Pan-African Association

The group voted on a number of important policies and established a new organization, the Pan-African Association. The objectives of the new organization would be:

1. to secure civil and political rights for Africans and their descendants throughout the world;
2. to encourage friendly relations between the Caucasian and African races;
3. to encourage African peoples everywhere in educational, industrial, and commercial enterprise;
4. to approach governments and influence legislation in the interests of the black races; and
5. to ameliorate the condition of the oppressed Negro in Africa, America, the British Empire, and other parts of the world.[11]

The delegates from the United States continued to play a key role in the new organization. Anna J. Cooper was elected to the executive committee and W.E.B. Du Bois was elected to lead the United States delegation.[12]

1919 Pan-African Congress in Paris

What has been referred to by some as the first Pan-African Congress was held February 19 through 21, 1919 in the Grand Hotel of Paris. As with the 1900

London Congress, both women and African-Americans continued to play major roles. The executive committee for the Congress consisted of M. Blaise Diagne (Senegal), President; W.E.B. Du Bois (U.S.A.), Secretary; Ida Gibbs Hunt (U.S.A.), and M.E.F. Fredericks.[13] Fifty-seven delegates from fifteen countries attended, including the president of Liberia.

1920 International Convention of the Negro Peoples of the World in New York City

The largest and most effective Pan-African Congress was held in New York City by Marcus Mosiah Garvey and his Universal Negro Improvement Association (U.N.I.A.) beginning August 1, 1920 and continuing for thirty days in Madison Square Garden. Unlike the other conferences that were held in the twentieth century, Garvey's convention reached into and attracted the masses. All of the other conferences were primarily directed to and attended by intellectuals and elites, with the exception of the Manchester conference in 1945. At the end of the convention that drew over 25,000 people, the Declaration of Rights of the Negro Peoples of the World was issued. In addition, the convention called for the creation of a Provisional Government of the African Republic and elected Marcus Garvey as Provisional President.

The Garvey convention was a direct outgrowth of a movement that began in Jamaica in 1914 and quickly spread throughout the world. At the heart of the movement was the philosophy of Garveyism, which preached Black nationalism and African repatriation. Garvey explained his vision on repatriation:

"We are not preaching any doctrines to ask all the Negroes to leave for Africa. The majority of us may remain here, but we must send our scientists, our mechanics, and our artisans, and let them build railroads, let them build the great educational and other institutions necessary."[14]

The goals of the U.N.I.A. were clear. Garveyites wanted:

1. The white man out of Africa
2. A free, independent, united Africa
3. Africa under the control of African people
4. Black professionals to pool their resources for the benefit of Africa
5. Strong organizations

The U.N.I.A. would provide the leadership for obtaining these goals. Therefore, it adopted a slogan that would make clear to all its objectives: "Africa for the Africans, those at home and those abroad;" an anthem: "Ethiopia, Thou Land of Our Fathers," and a flag with the colors of red, black, and green.

Garvey encouraged Africans in the diaspora to partake of the U.N.I.A. businesses and organizations, such as the Black Star Line, The Black Cross Navigation and Trading Company, Negro Factories Corporation, The African Legion, African Motor Corps, Black Flying Eagles, and The Juvenile Corps. Through the Black Star Line the following ships were bought: S.S. Frederick Douglass, S.S. Booker T. Washington, S.S. Antonio Maceo, and The Philis Wheatley. For those who were skilled in literary matters, they would work on several publications, *The Negro World* (1919), published in Spanish, French and English, weekly; *The Negro Times* (1922) published daily; and *The Black Man* (1933) published monthly.

Despite these important gains brought about by Garveyism, several of the leaders of the Pan-African elites sided with the United States Government in bringing false charges against Garvey that ultimately led to his conviction on felony charges and deportation back to Jamaica. Through covert actions by the United States Government, U.N.I.A. ships were sabotaged. The State Department called Garvey "an undesirable and indeed a very dangerous alien." Blaise Diagne, Senegalese and a member of the French Chamber of Deputies and the so-called Committee of Eight orchestrated a "Garvey Must Go" campaign. In their letter to the United States Attorney General on January 15, 1923, they wrote: " . . . The U.N.I.A. is composed chiefly of the most primitive and ignorant element of West Indian and American Negroes . . . In short, this organization is composed in the main of Negro sharks and ignorant Negro fanatics . . . ."

Even the United States Communist Party, through George Padmore, a fellow West Indian and one of the leaders of the Pan-African Congress in Manchester, opposed Garvey, along with Cyril Briggs and W.A. Domingo. Padmore wrote of Garvey:

> "..Garvey is much more than a dishonest demagogue who has profited from the wave of revolutionary protest of Negro workers . . . Garvey is an agent of American imperialism . . . The Garvey ideology is the most reactionary expression of Negro nationalism. Negro workers should not be deceived . . . They must understand that the only road by which they can acquire their freedom and emancipation is by organizing their forces . . . and establishing an alliance with white workers . . . "

1921 Pan-African Congress in London, Brussels, and Paris

This Congress has been historically referred to as the second Pan-African Congress. It was held in three locations, in London, England from August 28 though 29; in Brussels, Belgium from August 31 through September 1; and in Paris, France, from September 4 through 5. One hundred and ten delegates attended from thirty-eight countries. M. Blaise Diagne, who opposed Garvey, continued to serve as president with W.E.B. Du Bois serving as executive secretary.

1923 Pan-African Congress in London and Lisbon

What is referred to as the Third Pan-African Congress was held November 7 through 8 in London and on November 25th in Lisbon. A group known as The Circle of Peace and Foreign Relations coordinated the conference. Mrs. A.W. Hunton served as Chairperson of the Circle. While the number of delegates was small compared to earlier conferences, the Congress continued to draw prominent whites such as H.G. Wells.[15]

1927 Pan-African Congress in New York City

This conference on American soil, under the leadership of Mrs. A.W. Hunton and the chairmanship of W.E.B. Du Bois, drew a healthy contingent of African-American scholars, such as Rayford W. Logan, Charles H. Wesley, and Leo W. Hansberry. Melville Herskovits and approximately 5,000 other individuals attended, with 208 delegates. The following general resolution was adopted:

Negroes everywhere needed:

1. A voice in their own government
2. Native rights to the land and its natural resources
3. Modern education for all children
4. The development of Africa for the Africans and not merely for the profit of Europeans
5. The re-organization of commerce and industry so as to make the main object of capital and labor the welfare of the many rather than the enriching of the few
6. The treatment of civilized men as civilized despite differences of birth, race, or color

1945 Pan-African Congress in Manchester, England

This conference, considered by many to be the most important, was convened by Amy Jacques Garvey and others. She, Harold Moody, Du Bois, and Paul Robeson had hoped to have the conference in London.[16] However, Manchester was chosen after the idea was raised by Black colonial workers attending the World Federation of Trade Unions (WFTU) that was meeting in London.

It was here in Manchester that Dudley Thompson met and deliberated with individuals from Africa and its diaspora who would make monumental contributions to the African world. The committee, charged with organizing the Congress, was from all regions of Africa and its diaspora: Peter Milliard (British Guyana), George Padmore (Trinidad), Kwame Nkrumah (Gold Coast), Jomo Kenyatta (Kenya), and Peter Abraham (South Africa).[17] In Manchester, Thompson would meet these men and women whom he would later assist in the creation of African nationalism and statehood. In particular, Nkrumah and Kenyatta would work directly with Thompson in their respective countries, Ghana and Kenya.

At the conference, Nkrumah and Kenyatta discussed the critical problems facing Africa. Nkrumah led a session on "Imperialism in North and South Africa" and Kenyatta led a session on "The East African Picture." T. Ras Makonen, who was secretary of the Pan-African Federation, gave a paper on "Ethiopia and the Black Republics."[18] The overall tone of the conference was one of militancy, of the need for Africa and its diaspora to oppose imperialism through all means, including "positive action," which was interpreted to mean nonviolence.[19] From this conference emerged a plethora of seminal ideas that led to the creation of several progressive publications: Nkrumah's *Towards Colonial Freedom* (1947), Padmore's *How Russia Transformed Her Colonial Empire* (1946), and *Pan-Africanism or Communism? The Coming Struggle for Africa* (1956). These publications and the men and women who created and nurtured them would begin the long road to African political independence that would draw upon the skills and talents of Dudley Thompson and Bill Sutherland, two committed Pan-African activists.

Unlike many of the Pan-African leaders of the past, with the exception of John Brown Russwurm, Thompson and Sutherland were able to lend their substantial skills to efforts to create and sustain African political institutions on the continent. Thompson's work was primarily in East Africa (Kenya and Tanzania), while Sutherland worked in Dar es Salaam, Tanzania, from 1964 through 2001. Both men worked with African leaders who were engaged in Pan-African Movements, particularly in 1945. The following interviews will reveal the extent of their contributions. Thompson worked to insure that sound political and constitutional safeguards were incorporated into the governmental systems of Kenya and Tanzania after serving in the colonial British Air Force in World War Two. Sutherland, on the other hand, refused to serve in the war due to his pacifist beliefs that stemmed from deep religious and non-violent convictions. Nevertheless, both men were influenced by the leading Pan-African thinkers of the 50's, such as George Padmore, and consequently served Africa at a time of great need.

NOTES

1. Tony Martin, *The Pan-African Connection: From Slavery to Garvey and Beyond* (Dover: The Majority Press, 1985), page vii.

2. Peter Tosh, "An African."

3. James Baldwin, *The Fire Next Time* (New York: Laurel, 1963).

4. Julie Winch, *Philadelphia's Black Elite,* "Activism, Accommodation, and the Struggle for Autonomy, 1787 to 1848" (Philadelphia: Temple University Press, 1988), page 31.

5. Sheldon H. Harris, *Paul Cuffe: Black America and the African Return* (New York: Simon and Schuster, 1972), page 77.

6. Harris, page 83.

7. Esedebe P. Olisanwuche, *Pan-Africanism: The Idea and Movement, 1776-1991*, Second Edition, (Washington, D.C.: Howard University Press, 1994), page 26.

8. Esedebe, page 39. It is fascinating to see Booker T. Washington interested in movements of this nature because at the time, he was considered one of the strongest supporters of integration. His support of American racist social systems drew significant opposition from key African-American intellectuals and activists, such as W.E.B. Du Bois, William Monroe Trotter, and Ida B. Wells.

9. Esedebe, page 40 to 41.

10. Esedebe, page 41to 42.

11. Esedebe, pages 44 to 45. The following individuals were elected to leadership positions in the new organization: Bishop Alexander Walters (President), Henry Sylvester Williams (General Secretary), and R.J. Colenso (General Treasurer).

12. Esedebe, page 45.

13. *Crisis,* "The Pan-African Congresses: The Story of a Growing Movement," October 1927.

14. Tony Martin, *Race First,* "The Ideological and Organizational Struggles of Marcus Garvey and the Universal Negro Improvement Association" (Dover: The Majority Press, 1976). This is one of many works on Garvey by Professor Martin.

15. *Crisis.*

16. Esedebe, page 137.

17. Esedebe, page 138.

18. Esedebe, page 141.

19. Esedebe, page 144.

Ambassador Dudley J. Thompson

EARLY LIFE AND DEVELOPMENT

I was born in Panama and came to Jamaica when I was about nine, ten. My brother named Carl was older than me. Five boys, three girls. My brother did not take a similar path in his life as mine. We were very close but he, when I went to study teaching, he went and studied pharmacy. We grew up close together then but we were all together, we were always great playmates.[1] I went to school normally at home in Jamaica by my father, who was a school teacher. I was with him at his home and at an elementary school in Westmoreland, his school, Chantilly School, for the last two years, more or less at home. After that, I won a scholarship and went to the Mico Training College. And that was about 1935, '36, I think it was. '35? Could be '35. I got a scholarship there from the government, which is granted to the first five people who took the examination on the island, the Island Examination. They are called Pupil Teachers Examination. Candidates took it all over Jamaica and the first five got a scholarship to go to the Mico Training College or to the Women's Shortwood Training College. And I was second in those five. At that time Mico Training College was purely, singularly male. It was an unusual institution in that you can consider it, and I still do consider it, the "poor country black man's university." Most of the people came up from the country. It was not in the big league like the Ivy League and the big five here. You had Wolmers, you had Calabar, you had Jamaica College, you had Hampton. Those were for wealthy people, largely white, but not entirely. These are colonial days, remember. Rich white Jamaicans and wealthy people and city people, city folk. Country folk came up to these places to visit. Some went to Calabar. But the Mico was entirely a religious foundation. They went

11

along strongly in their religious non-denominational leanings. I spent three years at Mico. That was the full course of teacher training.

Life as a Teacher

And after three years there, I taught school in Jamaica in the country parts. I taught there for three and a half years or so as a headmaster in the various schools. I do remember that quite clearly. I felt my calling was to be a teacher and I still think it's been the most useful part of my life. I like teaching. The schools that I taught in after Mico were in the countryside outside of Kingston. They were country schools. But the first one was as an assistant. I didn't stay there for more than about two months and then I was able to take charge of my own school, as headmaster. Arriving in my own parish, I first taught at St. Mary in the country. And I remember quite well going to Albion Mountain near Jacks River. I remember people who were so kind to me going there. They were, setting me out in life as a young man, sort of organizing myself. Now, the first time in life you're going to think about the cost of living and things like furniture, laundry, etc. I was setting up house with their kind help. These schools were organized according to grades. A grade is the top school in Kingston, along down to D. I started at a C-grade school. And then I got an open invitation to teach in Enfield, Westmoreland, my own parish, which is where I grew up before I went to Kingston. I grew up in Westmoreland. I consider myself a member of that parish, my father's parish. And I went and taught at Enfield School there for the next two and a half years. I do remember going to a much better elementary school, after my two months as an assistant teacher in St. Mary. I became a first headmaster there. I can't forget that.

The first Sunday evening before I started school, a new school where I was going to start on Monday. I got out of bed that early morning and went over to that school room and I knelt down in that empty schoolroom, old schoolroom, smelling of bats' dung and chalk. I remember quite clearly kneeling down there and praying. I saw all the pictures on the wall and I prayed to God saying, "in the next few hours, young Jamaican men and women will be bringing their children over those hills and valleys all around us, putting their little children's hand in mine and saying, 'Teacher, see what you can do with this one for me.'" The picture I had seen when I prayed and I looked around the walls were the pictures of George I, George III, Henry II, Elizabeth and that sort of thing. And I took them all down and put up pictures of Marcus Garvey and some of the old leaders. Even one cut-out newspaper of a young man, a prominent black lawyer, N.W. Manley. I loved the teaching of children.

Color Consciousness

During the colonial days, color stratification was a reality as well. Light-skinned Jamaicans were able to assess positions, easier than darker ones. I first became aware of this social problem all the way in Panama. Instinctively, it was there because, being born in Panama and the Panama Canal Zone, you had the whites and the colored. At the place where I was born, you had the white American gold standard and you had this colored silver standard. I went to a colored school, for instance, and there was a white school. So I had all the assumed race sensitivity I'd say from my birth up. I got to knowing that there was this distinction between the whites, who got the best of everything. But I didn't harbor any resentment because I thought it was natural. Later on, of course, you found out how wrong it was.

You saw all sorts of discrimination as you grew up. So it wasn't the sort of Paul-on-the-way-to-Damascus revelation. I didn't even realize that the Jamaicans themselves practiced that type of color discrimination against each other, that, for example, if you're light-skinned, you got more access to privileges than if you were darker. Well, I didn't notice that until very, very late in the day because, in my mind, you are either a white or a black? And if you were in Jamaica, well, the planters, the big, rich plantocracy in Jamaica was all white and you could see them. They were the rich white men that rode horses or rode in buggies when black people walked. But I didn't notice the shade difference at all very much until I went to England. During the war, you noticed that people who thought they were white in Jamaica, when they went to England, they were classified as black. And it was then perceived with a certain degree of humor. In fact, there was a case, a letter, famous letter, written by a young WAAF, Women's Auxiliary Air Force, a woman who was coming home to Jamaica to be discharged. And she was complaining how all the time she had been treated improperly and just because she had one drop of black blood in her, she was discriminated against. Wee drop. And from that, you had the Wee Drop syndrome. The Wee Drop was a name stigma, a person who was complaining that they should have passed as white. But I didn't notice it very much until then.

I do not believe that color played any role whatsoever in helping me gain access to the Royal Air Force. I mean, the fact that I was a brown Jamaican. My degree of brown made me just black. I was just on the black side of the line. They didn't have any difficulty with me. The Americans are quite open in that with them you're either white or black. I'm black. My color is clearly black; no question of passing or anything like that. Never occurred to me anyway.

World War II

And then World War II broke out and everything else went in the background. You understand, it has nothing to do with Pan-Africanism because we were a colony; we were a straight uninformed colony. We heard stories of Hitler advancing through Europe and threatening London and other English cities back there, I joined the Royal Air Force in London.

As a teacher I was a part of Colonial Service, a part of the civil service in the country. But I left it. I resigned that job and went to fight, going to fight with Britain. In fact, I remember when I made up my mind to go and fight. We were getting news all the time about England getting her first battering, you know 1939. And I remember Coventry Hospital being bombed. It really felt, at that time, as a colonial, with the Union Jack as our flag, I felt some sense of loyalty to the motherland, as she was then. And I felt I had a duty to do something about it. And one day, I was in a dentist's chair, I remember now clearly, East Queen Street at Dentist Lloyds, and I picked up one of these books, these magazines that people keep in their reception with the magazines. It turned out to be *Mein Kampf.* And I opened it just by chance; God works in a mysterious way. I opened to the part where Hitler was giving the Jews and dogs and Negroes hell. I think we were described as something like semi-developed anthropoids or something like that. I was really stung by that. I really said, now, "This man's gone too far." This was the beginning. It struck me. I said, "Look, I'm going to join up." And in my youthful exuberance said "I'm going to get into a plane and I'm going over there and shoot down one of their planes to show them who is boss."

I went and signed up overseas and joined the Royal Air Force in England. The Air Force was not fully integrated; I served along with other whites. But I did not know that there was a white discriminatory policy in the forces in England. Growing up in Jamaica, we got to feel that this color prejudice was limited to America and the South of America and that the British didn't have it. We felt rather proud that we were British that we didn't have that sort of thing, as we thought at the time. Of course, it was so well hidden behind, I mean, you know the way they did it. They didn't tell you about it; they just left you there. And it was not easy to get in. Many of my friends that I saw afterwards, men who had tried to join at that stage of the war, because Britain thought they were going to win this war in about two years or so, you know were rejected. And they didn't need as many black people as volunteers. We had people there, Adolph B.A., the head of the extramural studies of the West Indies; he was turned down. And Moody's son, Dr. Moody's son, was turned down; born in England, English wife, English mother, and ROTC, that sort of thing. He was turned down and so was Dr. Marsh. All of these were turned down because there was a qualification: you had to be of "pure

European descent." Pure European descent that meant pure white. And they were turned down on those grounds. When I was there lining up to join there was this room where I had to answer all these various questions: religion, name, where you were born and so on. I came across this question: "Are you of pure European descent?" And I said "yes." When they came in and asked for me, I remember there was a sergeant, a peacetime English sergeant, big mustache, lots of medals, you know the "Poona" type. He came right down. "Did you see this Number 23 question? Did you understand what is written on that 23rd question?" So I stood up to my full five foot seven, you know, to this big giant of a man, "What makes you believe that I do not understand the English language?" It shook him, of course. He said, "Well, are you of pure European descent?" I said, "Yes. Test it here, take a blood test. Take a blood test now and find out if I am." Well, he couldn't cope with that. He simply waved his hand and I went through that part of his test. But it was very, very prejudiced at that stage. I didn't know until much years later how prejudiced the forces were. They were not just prejudiced to admit black people in but they were prejudiced further when it came to promotions and there were specific orders that they should not admit and commission us to become officers. I have got quite a lot of documentation on this. There's a book written quite recently called *"Our War,"* written about three years ago, I think, by an Englishman, Christopher Somerville published in 1998 in United Kingdom, ISBN 0297816683. *"Our War"* which tells you a lot of the difficulties they had at that time.

When I went into the Royal Air Force I didn't know how many other Jamaicans, black or colored were in the Royal Air Force. We wouldn't know. Even at the end of the war, they didn't list them, they didn't classify them, you see, because they were not supposed to be there at all. There's no classification. But I would say, when the group went over, there was twenty-five of us, and five of us got into the Royal Air Force. The others joined the Army. It was easier. You see, Air Force is a sort of elite place and not only is it elite, after that, you have the elite of the elite because, in the Air Force, you have the ground crew and the air crew and the elitist of the elitist of the elitist is the air crew officers. As you went up the tests became more difficult. And I made up my mind. I'm going to pass all those examinations. I'm going to come first in every one of them so they would have no excuse. They have the ground examinations, you know, in navigation and that sort of thing, which I was really ready for, and the other tests, administration and actual flight. I just had to come first, second, or third so there would be no excuse at all for not recommending me further up the ladder.

First I went to an initial training wing, where I got into the force. One day you're there, a civilian, and the next day you're an Army man. And it's a big difference, a huge jump. The man sitting down on his bench and yeah, you talk with him today and the next day when you're sitting down, you stand up and you stand to attention. And you're used to giving orders; now you're going to receive orders. And you feel yourself a part of a very big, big family group, a cog in a big organization, sometimes comfortable, sometimes not so comfortable. And the war was sticky in England. It was now, I think, about 1940, '41. Earliest days, I remember, we had to sleep in air raid shelters in the street. Because London was being bombed nightly I received initial training on the ground, then after that you had an elementary flying training school at a training airdrome and after that you went to an operational training unit, which was kind of a college. I went to the RAF Cranwell College, which is their finest college, Cranwell. It's like America's West Point in the RAF. I went there and I passed through and I got my wings and I joined air crew, on to a squadron for operational training and combat exercises.

Then I went into a squadron. They moved me from squadron to squadron where I did special duties. I was an officer. If you weren't an officer, you qualify by going to Cranwell and passing through there. And I was granted a commission as a Pilot Officer. It was unusual for a Jamaican to become an officer in the Royal Air Force. It was very rare, because there were others who were there before me, white fellows and some of whom had died, in fact; others who were there before me and very few of them ever made the grade of an officer, very, very few. They made a flying grade, they became a sergeant, flight sergeant and so on, with crew, an air crew, but very few of them were made officers at that time. The policy changed because the war was a long while taking place.

There was a dispute between the War Council, Army Council, and the Colonial Office. Because there had been a lot of disturbance in the colonies a lot of government and colonial officers were pressed at home. Churchill himself intervened at one stage as Secretary of the Navy and said that there should be no prohibition in law to prevent, by means of color bar or otherwise, to prevent black people, et cetera. He made his own intervention, although noting that he did not want to move too quickly, and that law was passed. In fact, I haven't got it with me here now but it was passed the same day by unanimous decision in the House of Lords and the House of Commons. But they didn't implement it. They made all sorts of oppositions. You either failed the medical or you failed the disposition or you failed that. Many years after that, we were still having the same hurdles until very late into the war. Finally in 1943 when the King's Regulations were reversed, the Naval Recruiting Regulations still stated that "black and coloured boys and any person in whom there is evidence of such parentage or ancestry are absolutely ineligible from entry unless by special sanction of the admiralty." Blacks were practically excluded from the Navy. In

1941 an advertisement appeared in "*The Scotsman.*" "Women between the ages of 18 and 40 are invited to enlist for general services overseas in the Army Tactical Service (ATS). They must be British subjects of pure European descent."

Norman Manley as Mentor

Norman Manley had been a hero for me as a young man. He was a lawyer and a Rhodes Scholar. And a soldier. He also joined in the Army in the First War, was decorated, actually. I knew him very well and he had a strong influence on me. I admired him even before I knew him because I used to read about his exploits in the newspapers and his great cases, which you heard about. I looked upon him as a great black man. When you think of Rhodes Scholar you don't think of Rhodes, we think of Norman Manley. He was the bright, brilliant, the best lawyer we've probably had up to this day, and a man who cared for people. He was a brilliant lawyer who was now going to do something else. I admired him. Everybody at my age, at the time did. I think I admired him as a model to be followed. I never imagined that I would follow in his footsteps. Never. Never in a month of Sundays. And I tell you something, here was a man who, like myself, became a Queen's Counsel as he did. I never dreamt any of those things. And when I left Oxford, when I got my degrees and I was deciding whether I should come home or get married, I got a letter from him in 1945 stating that he was about to leave behind his law practice and go in whole-time for politics. And that, if I cared to, there was a room in his chambers that I could come and work there. I thought this was heaven. I never, ever dreamt that in a month of Sundays I would get the honor to work with such a great man. Fortunately for me, I thought it over for several days and I felt I can go home as a lawyer, Manley's lawyer, working in his office, fantastic! I would be rich in a few years. I would be rich but after that, what? There was nothing else and I was so young. And I said, is there something missing? And I looked at my skin and I said, you know, all my training, by that time I'd been to Oxford, everything I had was Western. And there's nothing, no black training in me at all, no African training in me at all. And I looked at myself and I said, I must find out more about my black inside. I had felt the call of the blood, just thinking about it. And I decided to go to Africa where I would learn about it. So I didn't accept or take up the offer. And instead, after some cogitation and thought and pushing I went to Africa instead.

Pan-African Mentors

My friends in England at that time, friends like George Padmore who was a strong Pan-Africanist, had perhaps more influence than Manley upon me.

During the latter parts of the war, I got involved in the early Pan-Africanist movement. I met men like T.R. Makonnen, Jomo Kenyatta, Peter Abrahams and George Padmore. And then there was Kwame Nkrumah and there was Jomo Kenyatta as a student. And I met the other West Indian students there, while I was in the military, while I was still in the uniform. Now, you would think that would pose a problem for me. I was in the military, yet hanging around with these intellectuals who were radicals. There was no problem but Padmore, who was the brightest (and I don't think that man has ever got the praise that he's entitled to) was the mentor of us all, including Kwame Nkrumah and even C.L.R. James. He, Kwame, and T.R. Makonnen were planning the Fifth Pan-African conference there. When he was planning it and they said, look, the first day it was going to be opened, Kwame Nkrumah was supposed to come over but was not here, then he had some difficulty with the Nigeria/Cameroons at that time. And he couldn't come over on that plane in time and George, turning to me said would you chair the meeting? I was very young. Will you chair the meeting? I said, no, I can't do that, man. I'm in the Army. See, I'm wearing a uniform. Take off the jacket and the hat and . . . . Everybody come as they are. We don't see you as an Air Force man. So I stayed there for the first day and I shuffled up to the table and, fortunately for me, Mrs. Garvey, the first wife, she was pushing forward; she wanted to be chairman. I said, now, look, you run the show. So I said start there, as I'm nondescript in my trousers alone, I mean, no uniform. It didn't reveal me being in the Army. It could have been a difficulty at that point, I suppose. I got together with Padmore and Azikiwe.

After the war, well, toward the end of the war, they sent for me. The Jamaica government sent for me to come and help them to work with a plan for the resettlement of ex-servicemen. So I was seconded to the Colonial Office and I worked in the Colonial Office in London for some time. And then I went over to Jamaica. I asked for another Jamaican to come with me, Bunting, who was a flying man from the good old Biggin Hill days. He was a pilot officer and he just got his commission. And I took him over, his English wife and myself. We went to Jamaica to settle down the ex-servicemen and we stayed there for some time working on the plans for them. That was '46 to '47, end of the war then.

And when I had been in London, I was with Padmore and the others in the last part of 1944 and 1945 and I actually could see them quite a bit because while I was at Oxford, I used to come down almost every weekend to attend law lectures and attend my law training at Gray's Inn. So I met them, well, two, three times a week. And I always spent a lot of time with George Padmore. I remember one particular occasion, while I was up there with him at 22 Cranleigh Gardens and when he introduced me to all this socialist literature and so on, things of which I had never become aware at all. He opened my eyes because he could read the British Empire like his hand, like he would read a book. So you could see all sorts of people coming to the scene there, Ho Chi Minh, everybody would be coming in there as young revolutionaries.

And I was up there with him one day. Ho Chi Minh was earning money as a postman, dropping postcards and so on. And when I came down, I would stay in London and I would see them. And on this occasion, George said, "By the way, look, I just got a cable from C.L.R. James. He's a great friend of mine. He's in New York in America. And the cable says that I am to meet a young African coming out and the cable says, will you go to meet him at Waterloo Station at such and such a time?" He just asked would I like to go and meet him when he's there. So I said sure. So I jumped up and went with him. When we reached there, I saw this handsome young African sitting on his grip, as he called it then, sitting there waiting for us, handsome young man. Right. And he gave George the letter from C.L.R. It was then that George read it, then smiled and put it in his pocket. He showed me afterwards, "This man is assured that he wants to drive the British out of his country, Gold Coast. He may well succeed." But postscript, "he is not very bright." The letter was there. But the two of them hit it off immediately. The chemistry just flew between them. They're just naturals. George Padmore and Kwame Nkrumah. After that, I listened like the young one, walked around with them, fetching this and that. And we had a small group, including Jomo Kenyatta, George Padmore, Kwame Nkrumah, Azikiwe, and Peter Abrahams. Azikiwe was writing some newspapers in Nigeria but who came over now and again. W.E.B. Du Bois made one or two appearances. I only saw him; I didn't have anything to do with him at that time, until later on. And then there was T.R. Makonnen, there was Peter Abrahams, the South African writer. There was this other man who became president, a doctor, Dr. Banda. I never got on with him. But the nucleus of that lot was Padmore, Kwame Nkrumah, Makonnen, and myself. We'd sit down there and sometimes at lunchtime, because between us there was not much money, not much pocket money. Padmore is getting about five pounds a week as a newspaper writer from *Amsterdam News* or some black newspaper. Jomo is a roving electioneering man, campaigning. And I was a student. But I had a study job. I had credit. So I could buy the lunches. They'd chalk it up to me. And we'd all sit down together and eat.

And one day I saw one of the RAF planes fly over. I remember it as clear as I see today. RAF plane flew over and here was this young, handsome African, Kwame Nkrumah, following it with his eyes, right along, right along. And then he said to us, "You know, one day I'm going to have planes like that flying over my country. But they're going to have my flags on it instead." I have never forgotten because it came to pass. He was not a dreamer, he was a visionary and a dedicated visionary. An activist, one of the greatest men I have seen come out of Africa. A real Pan-Africanist.

But of these two men, George Padmore and C.L.R. James, George Padmore had the most influence on my thinking. C.L.R. was a much deeper, much more profound thinker. He was really deep, big, a monument of an intellect. But George was a day-to-day man, arranger and organizer and a man whom I could understand better. You don't have to research what he's thinking. He can think along with you. He was nearer to my level than C.L.R. James. He looked up to C.L.R. C.L.R. was such a great mind that I couldn't help but follow up his way of thinking.

Employment in Jamaica

My contact with these great thinkers and activists changed abruptly when I was sent to Jamaica to settle ex-servicemen. I was in London with the Colonial Office and the Colonial Office sent me in uniform, as a member of the RAF, back to Jamaica. So I didn't have any choice about that at all.

When I was in Jamaica, before I came out of the service, the war was still on, dragging along in Japan and they're cleaning up a bit, although there was no actual fighting, the war was not declared over. I was in Jamaica. I'd settled as a liaison officer and there I applied for the Rhodes Scholarship. I was awarded a Rhodes Scholarship to go straight to Oxford.

PAN-AFRICAN ACTIVISM

Return to Europe: Oxford

So I came back to England in 1947 now to do my Oxford University training. After a short time there, I moved between Oxford and London because I did my law studies at the same time as I was getting my degree in jurisprudence. I was elected president of the West Indian Students' Union, WISU. And my copartner on the other side was the West African Students' Union, WASU, an even more strong political union, was Joe Appiah from Ghana. Joe Appiah. He was there. He was my friend. We were at college together and there are always difficulties with the Colonial Office. And I was still in uniform and I remember one occasion discussing the question, why is it that WASU and WISU couldn't get together. WASU actually was far more politically advanced than we were in the West Indies, far more political. We knew very little about Africa. WASU members were politicians. They were students, but also politicians from Africa, Ava Dankwe and Kwame Nkrumah. And I remember they were making a big fuss over the 1945 agreement and a declaration of 1945 as to what was going to happen after the war. It said something about being given freedom, that the colonies would be granted freedom. I think it described them as colonies, dependencies or whatever, would be given greater governance over themselves. And the students in Africa took it very seriously. We in the West Indies never really took it very seriously at all. We always, we were always compliant, aside from the few leading bright sparks, like, of course, Marcus Garvey always was and Manley always was. Most of us really just took it as, well, Britain says that she's going to help us until we are able to govern ourselves and then again, we are prepared to wait. But the Africans were not. They were very restless and rebellious. But you know WASU and WISU did not have much contact with African-Americans who like Du Bois came through there, and participated in the Fifth Pan-African Congress, during this period. There wasn't much interaction with either black servicemen in Europe or black students from the United States who were studying there. In fact, there were very few students. And I remember once, on one occasion, when we were, as club men meeting together, hearing some of the few black Americans, not officers, but non-commissioned officers, saying "But you know, I can't understand these African fellows. They can't even speak English." That was the attitude. I mean, complete ignorance. But we had very little to do with each other. Very little to do with Africa.

Pan-African Conference in 1945

Now, of course, Du Bois himself was different. When this Pan-African conference, of which I could say quite a lot because it was very important, when the Pan-African conference met in 1945 in Manchester, England, Du Bois was there but he didn't bring along with him the following he had promised. I questioned him because I was sitting up at the top table. I said, "What, well, you let us down. We don't have any money. We're running out of money." And he said, "There was a difference as to where the conference was to be held in the U.S.A. or U.K. or Africa. The N.A.A.C.P. promised support if it were held in the U.S.A. And I remember, this was the first conversation I had ever had with Du Bois. He said, "Look, it was the Devil's own job for me to get a passport to come here. I had to go to the president." But "I had to go to the president himself, personally and ask him, beg for a visa to come to this conference. And I was given a visa only to come to the conference and to report back immediately afterwards. The others couldn't come." But they were a bit disappointed because in the preparations for the conference, the weeks coming up to it, there was quite a lot of things to do because it was a big conference, the biggest ever arranged.

Moody wanted it in London and Du Bois wanted it to be in America. Azikiwe wanted it in Nigeria, saying, "It's an African conference; it must be in Africa." George manipulated and manipulated, did a good job of settling the dispute. He had it in Manchester, England, largely because Makonnen had enough money from his Manchester restaurants to hold it there and secondly, there was a huge international labor conference taking place in England at the same time, just before. And it had leaders, journalists, and activists there from all over the world, Sudan, Jamaica, all over the world, the black world. George Padmore arranged it. And most of those people would come down to the conference. And it was indeed a big and a different sort of conference from any of the prior Pan-African conferences. I would say, from day to day between 500 and 1000 people attended the Pan-African Conference. Probably more. And Padmore was the convener, the chair. He was the moving spirit, the organizer, although they gave him the title "Father of Pan-Africanism" he gave it to Du Bois. But I've heard Du Bois say, no, I am not the father; Padmore is the father. Neither of them, of course, coined the phrase; that was coined actually by a Pan-African lawyer, Sylvester. Mr. Sylvester Williams, actually a Trinidadian lawyer. It was George and Kwame who organized that very, very different Pan-African Conference in Manchester. It was different. There were activists; it was full of thinkers and doers. Before that, the conferences were sort of meetings complaining about institutional repression in England, about the incidents of prejudice and racial bigotry, et cetera. These took place everywhere. This was a different conference. One, it didn't have a usual white group of liberals who had helped us in the early days. It was an all-black conference and from then on, the blacks looked after themselves, and accepted their own responsibility in the Pan-African movement as one.

Secondly, it had a lot of working-class students and trade unionists and not just big intellectual elites at the university levels. A lot of the working-class people were there and they were very vocal, very vocal. Again there were only four, I think three independent countries. And those were Ethiopia, Liberia, Haiti and Egypt. The others like Jamaica, Barbados, Nigeria, Gold Coast were all colonies. Very few whites came to our Congresses and at that fifth conference, even fewer. English liberals made a few appearances and so on. I asked Du Bois why more members from the United States had not come and why the NAACP did not take any role in the conference. He said that they were not granted visas by the United States to come. Kwame Nkrumah led the conference. And I remember when he electrified that conference. And this was the first conference that came up with a direct aim. It wasn't just a complaining group. It came up with a specific aim of working on a strategy, a strategy for advancement of black people. And the key to it was given when Kwame Nkrumah got up. He was sitting about two seats away from me on a bench. And he got up and made a most electrifying speech. You could feel everyone there listening. You would hear a pin drop. He was on fire and just gave us a straight mandate. "Go back to your countries. Go back to your country and fight for political independence by all means that you have available. Seek ye first the political kingdom and then all good things will follow afterwards." That was his ringing message and it was in everybody's ears. And you could see the effect. You could feel the passion moving in all. I could see old Ken Hill from Jamaica. I could see quite a few Nigerians moving around. You see, Kwame Nkrumah himself was there giving his speech and there was Azikiwe. They were all leaders. They were all going back to fight for political independence. That fight got started after the '45 conference. And such was the effect that it was largely due to that movement. That within 18 years or so, you could say over 20 years after that '45 conference, that some 70 ex-colonies had their independence, including Jamaica, Trinidad, Barbados, you name it. Nigeria, all the big African countries, they got their independence within 20 years after that conference. Ghana led because she was way ahead.

As I sat there I also thought of Marcus Garvey and his movement. Marcus Garvey was the essential Pan-Africanist. But he was not officially attached to the movement. Sometime I would like to try and find out why because he was undoubtedly the greatest mass-mobilizer of all time. He was a greater mass mobilizer than Martin Luther King or anybody else, Farrakhan, anybody else. And that led him off from, when he unfurled that black UNIA flag, Universal Negro Improvement Association UNIA black nationalism. He got millions to follow him all over the world. Some of them were in Panama, some in Costa Rica, every where, every union group which he met at, he founded various caucuses and groups. He published newspapers. His wife was there. But he was not then fully appreciated. Garvey grew, grew in stature after his death, we know, later. He was accepted as a great leader but he was never given the value for his ability in his own lifetime. I always admired Garvey. I saw and was attracted to Garvey before I became a Pan-African because my father was a schoolmaster and therefore, an educated man compared to men like Marcus Garvey and looked down upon him socially. Garvey was looked down upon by the middle class. You know the difficulties he had in Jamaica. The white establishment treated him as a nuisance and opposed him. He was regarded as a troublesome nobody, until he began to speak. And then he had his following because Garvey spoke to the minds of a people who were subservient. And in fact Garvey could see the subservience right there. The whites had the blacks clearcut, while he gave to blacks courage to stand up. He spoke to their minds. He gave them a sense of self-value that no other leader had done before. And I used to steal away and go and listen to him at Edelweirs Park in Jamaica as a little boy. I didn't understand what he was talking about, of course. But there was something sincere about him. He was a man who was fighting for right and appealed to black people. He made them feel worthwhile. My father didn't like him at all. In fact, he had a lawsuit against him, something about not paying rent which my father won in court. So I was not on his side. But I did admire this man and later on, as things went on, I saw how great he was.

But Amy Jacques Garvey was at the Fifth Pan-African Congress. She took my chairmanship! She was recognized. In fact, I think they had to put down her name instead of mine for chairman in the first day because I couldn't do it officially. But she spoke well and she was, as usual, a firebrand. Not many, but there were some.

Development of Interest in Africa

I would say my interest in Africa leaked in from time to time. I remember hearing a Reverend Walter Brown who was a preacher in Kingston who had been a missionary out there, he had been a Jamaican teacher, went to the Mico. Then he was a parson and he went out as a missionary to Africa. And he went to the All Saints Church. He used to preach and I used to go out there sometimes on a Sunday. We would listen to him talk about Africa and it kindled a small spark within me somewhere. Yeah, it kindled a spark. So I really thought that there was something there I would like to know about. And then when Garvey spoke it blossomed. You know, the first thing I remember seeing, and this was before I could read, so to speak, the first I began to look through was *The Crisis* and that was a Du Bois publication. When I was about three years of age, my father took *The Crisis* regularly and I remember lying down on the floor while my father was reading and looking at these pictures. I couldn't read and I would show him the pictures of these men that were in it, the black Americans, men and women who had been so successful, millionaires, professionals driving motorcars. There was a Madame Walker, who became a cosmetology millionaire from her cosmetology. And I remember showing him one and saying, "Who is this man, Daddy? Who is this man?" I was quite a bit of a nuisance, most of the time, showing him these black people who had been successful. Well, we didn't have anybody like that down in Panama or in Jamaica. And he said, "Oh, that is Dr. Carver. He's a bright man. He invented peanut butter and several other things." Oh-ho! That, the peanut butter alone was enough for me. That made him a great man. But we had the connections from time to time, something black that attracted me because it was like a part of you.

But that was sort of a general sense of blacks and their achievement, particularly in America. But specifically Africa? When did I become aware of Africa as the homeland of African people? Well, I'll tell you. After I qualified as a teacher in 1951, I was in England and married my wife from Trinidad and I'd had a daughter and I was living in the suburbs in England at Waterhouse. I was deciding where I was going to practice. I was in the very good chambers of, not Sir Hugh Foote, but his brother, Dingle Foote, who was a Queen's Counsel, a well-known British barrister who later became Solicitor General for England. A wonderful, liberal family. There's a very liberal family in England called the Footes and the brother, Sir Hugh Foote, is one of the best governors we have ever had. I was in his chambers in London and I was working there. And then it was at that time I saw a lot of the Pan-Africans, Padmore and the others, and they were persuading, they later persuaded Kwame Nkrumah to go back to Ghana. And Kenyatta to go back to Kenya. He had come to study law but Padmore persuaded him not to continue studying law, to go to Africa and to fight for independence with the other people, that he was going to do political party work. And we had meetings regularly every week; also read about Africa. And Kenyatta left. I was very attached to Jomo, very attached to him, and we suddenly didn't hear anything at all; he was just cut off. He couldn't get any messages. George was just sending letters and not receiving replies. He used to be our post office and he was the man who would tell us what has happened in Kenya. What is happening all over Africa. We wouldn't know anything else except what came through George Padmore who I think founded the African Institute for International Affairs, in which, I think Dr. Williams became one of the secretaries to that publication. I know C.L.R. James also did become a secretary to that institute, African Institute for International Affairs. He sent out papers, distributed papers telling people all about the Garvey movement and about the African movement. And he said to me, you know, you should go over to Africa. You're going into this practice, right? Why don't you go to Africa and practice? So I would think about Africa. And then they said, "You could find out first what's happening to Kenyatta. He left us here. We haven't heard anything else from him for a long time. And you go out." He sort of pushed me along that track. But I had a son, my son was born in London and he was very ill. He had asthma and all the diseases you could think about, asthma, pneumonia, and all pulmonary diseases. The doctor said we should go to a dry country. And they somehow worked out that the slopes of Kilimanjaro would be the place. And then that was again Tanganyika, which was just south of Kenya. And from what we had learned, George's friend, very much in touch, Kenya was a powder keg. So that's the place to go and study it. So I decided then to take an interest in the country and to start my practice there.

And I put both feet in it. I went out to the country not knowing a word of the language with a family of two children.

I knew that once I got admitted to the bar, I had to have that to begin with, but after I got it, I'd have to practice to qualify and each country had its own criteria. Tanganyika is where I was going at the time and hoping to practice and make a living. I was told I'd need six months before I could practice. Six months of apprenticeship, then apply to the government. You just have to decide on that you were going to be a lawyer for the society and for six months you didn't pass any more exams or anything. At the end of six months you would qualify, you apply, on the British qualification.

Law Practice in East Africa

So I went down there, signed up for my six months and used that six months to study the language, which was Swahili and a couple of other African languages. And I studied the politics of the situation, because Tanganyika was very different from Kenya. The two of them were worlds apart, although they had a long shared border. Tanganyika was trusteeship territory and you had more Europeans settling down there, that is Italians and Germans and French and Greeks. Although you treated them all as white European people, who were more friendly, as distinct from Kenya, where you had the British and South African and you had strict prejudice in Kenya which you didn't have in Tanganyika. Tanganyika prided itself that it didn't have that prejudice, they thought. Until I tried to send my daughter to the white school down there later on. That's another story. But in Kenya, you had apartheid as strict as you had in South Africa. Oh, yes. The moment you crossed that border, you saw the difference, white plantocracy with a heavy hand.

Law Practice in Tanganyika

I met Julius Nyerere I think it was '50 or '51. I had been practicing and had a very good practice in Tanganyika because it had all white doctors for all the white officers. I was the only black lawyer there, which didn't mean much because Africans didn't have much money and whatever they had they gave. But they came in flocks and gave me a good practice in the law courts when I had my six months over. One day while I was there, I had to establish my own office under great difficulty because my house I had in England I had to sell everything and plunge everything into this African venture.

One day, my clerk came to me and said, "Bwana, there's a gentleman outside waiting to see you with the others but he said let the others go before him because he wants to talk to you after everybody's gone." I said fine. So when the last client left out, he brought in this small, ordinary looking man. There is nothing outstanding about Nyerere's appearance. Small, little Chaplin mustache sort of thing and he sat down. He said he was a teacher. He had come back quite recently from Edinburgh, where he had gone to study, and he was a teacher in one of the schools near the Northern lakes. And he was talking some politics to his people around there in the hope of starting a party and the management in the school told him that if he didn't stop interfering in politics they were going to fire him. He was afraid of losing his job and he wondered if legally he had any protection to stand on. He wanted some advice. And he was poor, he didn't have any money. He had a big family and couldn't afford to lose his job. So, just talking to him, you could find that this is a very different sort of man. You didn't need to spend more than ten minutes talking to him to realize that this is just not an ordinary African you're talking to, a man of unusual ability and vision. So I said, "How much time have you got?" He said, "Well, I was hoping that I'd be able to go back tonight to my classes on Monday. I have to go to church." And I said, "Well, would you like to spend a weekend with my family?" He was glad and overjoyed to do that. So he came with me to my home and I think we practically talked nonstop for almost the whole of that weekend.

I saw his vision. I listened to what he spoke about in Africa and he was so much on the ball. The vision made me think wider than I ever thought before because Tanganyika was just a group of different communities; it wasn't a country. They spoke in about 150 different languages and different tribal groups, having nothing to do with each other and none of them very rich, no money or other resources. All small districts. And this man had a vision of welding the whole of that place into one powerful country with one language, Swahili. And this young teacher, without any money or support worked out the fact that he was going to form this political party which he had in his mind. And I said, my advice to you is, "Organize and organize and organize." He left with a gift, my secondhand typewriter that I had there on the table and my secretary, an unusual African young woman. Bright, bright. Lucy Lameck who later became one of his ministers. And I promised to pay her salary for two years while he organized.

He went back home without a cent in his pocket, just transport money home and a vision in his mind and a dedication in his heart. A tremendous man. And in less than no time he formed the Tanganyika African Nationalist Union. On that typewriter we had worked out a rough sketch of the first constitution of TANU, T-A-N-U, Tanganyika African National Union. The manuscript is still somewhere in the archives of the Union Building, with the typewriter. I think it's still there. They had an archive and a museum of the formation of the party in Dar es Salaam. I believe it is still there. I'm not quite sure.

We typed the initial constitution out together. For I had little experience in the legal business, constitutional law, trade law and so on. We had a big difference in that he said only Africans would join this. And I told him, it's going to cost a lot. Politics costs a lot of money and you need a car. There's a big country to go around, going to need Jeeps, you're going to need secretaries. And my own Jamaican and English experience tells me, you will need help. And he said "No, no, it's going to be African, purely an African union. This is not to be anybody else because in Tanganyika, though we didn't have the prejudice you had in Kenya, you have what I describe as the Unholy Trinity of the Europeans at the top, the wealthy Indians in the middle, East Indians from India people, very wealthy, and the Africans, as usual, on the bottom." The Unholy Trinity. And he said, we do not want this. I said, there are some liberal Indians that I know, people who would think with us and who would damn sure grant you enough money to start with this. He said "No, this is going to be an African union." We split on that. I said, nevertheless, there you are. And he was boss. I followed him.

He had not started to grapple with the whole concept of Ujamaa at that point. That was to come. That was probably in his mind. He knew nothing about the ideology of Ujamaa. Probably it developed during the next fifteen months or so. He said he was going to go all over the country and organize. His manner was such that people would listen to him. He was a sincerely honest, modest man, a fatherly figure. His ways, his method of approach, anybody could go to Mwalimu. We called him Mwalimu, the "Teacher." And anybody could approach him. He would go right around and he collected people. Of course, the chiefs were against him. The big chief, the resident chiefs who were recognized by the United Kingdom.There was one from Nchara, Tom Maraeale.

But Nyerere was there. We gave him money to go to England to plead his cause before the Third Committee of the United Nations in New York. On one occasion, he went with some of his tribesmen to show what they were doing with them up there. But he was an eloquent speaker and he was received with such welcome arms in England and he spoke always for independence. He wanted independence. There was another big difference between Kenya and Tanganyika. Tanganyika was under the United Nations whereas Kenya was directly under the Colonial Office.

Another thing, when I met with Nyerere over the constitution, he always gravitated toward the one-party state. Where we started out, we had the strongest division on that point. And he called me, "Oh, you're an Oxford-trained man, you got to follow the Oxford people." And I said "No," but you want my sort of impression of democracy, the fundamental issues, you've got to have an opposition. And his point is, we will have the opposition within our party but we need a one-party state. And he discussed it but he was very, very firm on that. He changed it later on and when he changed it, he had to go on almost a hunger strike to get them to change it. It was so well fixed in their minds. He was firmly, firmly committed to this one-party state at that stage. But he was having some problems in Arusha. The colonial government arrested or moved, tried to move the people off the land. The Mwarusha tribe. He had to go to the United Nations to seek assistance. We gathered money to send him and one of the tribesmen. He made a very strong impression with them. They won the case. At least, he showed that it was a terrible imposition against the people. It took away their land. And the government said, as a reason for the removal, that they were over-grazing it with cattle. Whereas it was very good coffee land, very good coffee land. The Germans and British had essentially taken it away to give to the European settlers. They gave it to them and threw the people off but the Mwarusha had walked miles and came back. Eventually the government came in and put them in trucks and they took them away. Still the people came back. The next time, they burned down the huts of the people there, burned down their huts. And the people came back and dug holes, dug like a cave in the ground and moved in down there. They were that determined not to leave. They loved their land. I advised Nyerere on that, too. We prepared him properly to present all of these things. We didn't need to teach him to speak; he was an extremely eloquent speaker. But we threw him the political lines and then sort of, well, general representation, constitutional and legal points- Tanganikya was Trusteeship Territory and did not exist under a colonial office.

Nyerere was committed to some form of African socialism, Ujamaa. He wanted to make quite sure that he was not copying anybody else. He knew that the socialism as practiced in the outside world was not suited to us for all sorts of reasons. But he had the same idea, the central idea of socialism as an egalitarian community, just as I suppose you can say, community based on equality. The central theme, the whole center of equality. He had that in mind and it became "Ujamaa na Kazi," which meant Freedom and Work. And when he did things, he did it in such a big way that it really was understood and adopted by the entire country, took the whole country in. He established a political school. He established a school where all civil servants would go and learn the political ideology of the country. It was a good thing because it prepared for the next generation of leaders, which are still there. He did a lot to educate the whole country. What Nyerere did for Tanganyika can never be over-valued.

I spent nearly six years there practicing law, between Tanganyika and Kenya. When you qualified for one, you qualified for the other. One moved easily between Kenya and sometimes Uganda. A few cases in Uganda took me to that country. But most of my work was, the first part of it, in Tanzania, before we settled, made my office and my home.

Law Practice in Kenya

But I worked in Kenya when the Mau Mau started. I represented many of the freedom fighters from the beginning. One of my first big cases was one where some people came down, some Kenyan police came down from Kenya because they felt that Mau Mau had broken out and that it was going to spread from Kenya to Tanganyika. They hadn't a clue. And therefore they went to some of the white European farms and were arresting and interrogating, beating up a lot of African Kikuyus who had come down there to work, but the police thought they had come down there to spread Mau Mau. They beat some of them very, very badly.

Well, it's not English farmers you had down there, South African farmers; you had European farmers, the Greeks and the Germans and the French. Some Quakers. And they did not put up with this sort of thing at all. They complained about these people coming to beat them up and protected their own workers from them. And then one day I had a call from the District Commissioner, the regional officer, the one superior to the District Office, a high post for the post next to the governor in Tanzania, or Arusha. He wanted me to come there for a talk. He wanted me to defend the Kenya police who had been attacking the Kikuyus. I said, "What is this?" Because I was usually on the side of the Africans. I was anti all of that. My clients were persecuted Africans. But he wanted to speak to me. So I went up there, not knowing what is happening, drove up to his place.

Arusha is a beautiful city. It's a nice climate, houses built with bricks, for the permanent residence of English. There are trees, flowering and fruit trees and orchards and so on. And there was this huge, white palace for the district commissioner. I went to see him. He said, "Oh fine, make yourself at home." And after this formality he said, "Look, there's a peculiarity here. I'd like to explain this and we're going to ask you to defend some men. After I tell you the story, if you do not feel like defending them, there will be no hardship; I will understand. But I do hope that you would defend them because your name has gone abroad here and we established your reputation as a lawyer. I, as the provincial commissioner, have been asked to give these men the best possible defense that they can have. And I'm asking you if you would take a brief to defend." I asked "To defend who? Defend the policemen, the policemen that have come down, the Kenya policemen who had come down and beat up these people?" The European farmers filed cases against them, filed cases of brutality and also, other things, assault and grievous harm. Some of the Africans died. So these farmers are taking up their case and they wanted me now to defend these officers. "This is a reversal of my role," I said, "Well, you know, this is not my cup of tea at all."

And he said he understood and if I refused to accept it, he would understand the situation. And he was very, very civilized about it. He said he thought it would do him a lot of good if I were to defend them and to make it clear that at least they had the best defense available. But it wasn't only European, Africans that came down from Arusha. Their white officers came with them. So there were white officers and they had two or three white officers and about nine or so blacks who came down with them, who ran around and locked up Kikuyu in Tanganyika. It appears the brutality was clear. I said "I will consider this," and having considered this, I decided to take it and to use it.

I decided to take the case and I put my conditions in writing. One, that I would have no interference by the government or anybody else as to how I conducted the case. I was to have my own choice as to how I conducted the case. I had in my mind exactly what I was going to do. He agreed, paid me a reasonable fee. They were going to feel this one. And I took statements from all of these wretched policemen, African policemen from the north. I was not going to defend the white officers. I was not going to defend the white men. That was part of my conditions. The white officer would have to find his own defense and I would fight for the others. They didn't mind that. They had no idea what I was going to do. So he had his own lawyer, didn't really need one as it turned out. I had these others. I was defending the black ones who did the actual beating. I took a statement from each of them and I got their statements as to exactly what they did. They told me in full, they had acted on the orders of the boss to beat them. Sometimes they'd beat people on the soles of their feet until they were almost mad. They put ice, huge chunks of ice on their chests. It almost weighed them down and they took it off and put a bucket of hot water on them. They hanged them up by their toes. All sorts of tortures you could imagine, all sorts of bestialities took place. I wrote every account down and I got them to sign it and put their fingerprint on each one. Each one of them.

So when we went into this court at Arusha, Judge Biron, and I remember the Judge Biron, B-I-R-O-N. I remember him up to this day, the big, pronounced nose, Jewish extract. He greeted everybody, feeling very nice myself, and the attorney general doing the prosecution. So I am representing the black police. The white man didn't have any lawyer because he said he pleaded guilty. He wasn't even imprisoned, while the others, his juniors, were kept in jail, he was on bail, free. Even the prosecution did that to their own people. When he came into the court room, he came in almost like a hero. When the white people came in with him, he didn't sit down with the others or stay with the criminals. He sat in the court, the well of the court with the other white people. And he had pleaded guilty in a separate trial, sentenced to be deferred until the case of the others came up.

So the pre-arranged plan was, I would come up and plead guilty on all of these people and they were going to sentence them to one day in court, which means that they would be immediately free. That was the plan. So when they came up, the first man was called and on my instructions he pleaded not guilty. I was going to expose the whole show. So the judge looked at me very strangely. "I don't know what the hell you're talking about." You know, that sort of thing. Anyway, you'll find out. The second one came up, "Not guilty." The judge looked at me, you know, and looked at Attorney Elkhart. Because this was all agreed beforehand. The judge looked at me, the attorney general looked at me and they spoke together. The attorney general went up and spoke to the judge. And the judge said to me, "Mr. Thompson, are you sure you are giving your clients the best advice you can by pleading not guilty? Because the facts seem to be quite clear." I said, "The facts seem to be quite clear that they are not guilty and I want the facts to be put down quite clearly." So he says, with a shrug, "Well, I am going to let you carry on the case, you better consider what you're doing." When the third one came, I had about nine to come. The third one came up, "Not guilty." That was too much for them. They said, now look, the judge almost chewed up the table and said, "Look, I am going to take charge of this pleading because it's not going right. I am going to question the men myself." So when he, the fourth one, came up, he asked him, "Did you beat the man? Did you do this? Did you, according to the statement?" The man said "Yes." He says, "I'm going to put that down as guilty." I said, "No! No! No! according to the law, you must put it on in his own words! And the man would say he's not guilty." The judge said, "According to the law, the man says he's guilty. We are in Africa, you know?" The fifth man came up and he didn't get a chance to plead not guilty. "Did you beat this man? Did you do that, that, that?" And he said "Yes." "I'll put him down as guilty." So he put the whole down as guilty. Now, that would mean that if they are all guilty, he would sentence them to a day in prison, as they had all agreed beforehand, including the first two who had already pleaded on the record. Sentence them to a day so they could take the public transport and go back to Kenya and they would have no right of appeal. You can't appeal if a sentence is less than so many days. There's no right of appeal. It's final and done, good British justice! So I said, and what is more, since they, I couldn't appeal, I would not have a final word.

So I objected and so we argued the constitution, argued the legal procedures to a certain extent, and I began to make my own statement, which I asked to be recorded. It started and then when the facts were brought out, they stopped. I said, "I would like to put on record the fact that the first two men pleaded not guilty." The third one didn't have the chance to plead and I explained exactly what happened, as my speech, which should be recorded, so that the Court of Appeal would see what happened in this court. And I did expose the whole of it. That's exactly what happened, and sat down. They finished it. And the judges looked over at me and said, "I sentence all these men to a day in prison. Having spent more than their day in court almost, they can, they are now free to leave." Now, you know that my speech was not going up to the court of appeals because there is no grounds of appeal. The matter was done and finished and over, good British jurisprudence! That was the law in East Africa. And this is Tanganyika, not Kenya. Oh, Kenya was even worse. In Kenya, they'd probably cite me for contempt, many times.

On October 20, 1952, Jomo Kenyatta was detained by the British authorities, and on arrest wrote a note to the white arresting officer to give to me. He wanted me to defend him after he had been arrested. I was living in Moshi at the time in Tanzania. But I never got the message. I had warned Jomo several months before and several times that he was going to be arrested. It was quite clear to us that he would be arrested. And he usually laughed at that and said, "That's all right. If I'm arrested, I've got a good lawyer, you." Anyway, as soon as he had been arrested, he was quick to send the note, immediately sent a note to me because he knew I would do what I could. So I knew he was going to do that. And when they arrested him at gunpoint in his bed, after they took him out of his bed, he scribbled a note. He told me afterwards, it's in green ink; he says he used green ink. Scribbled it on the back of an envelope which was nearby: "Send to Moshi, for my lawyer, Dudley." And the Englishman who was in charge of them took it and put it in his pocket; he had these big, wide safari pockets. And what happened to it, nobody knows. When I heard it over the air that he was detained, not that he was arrested but that he was detained, I immediately sent a wire to the Attorney General, stating that I requested to see my client, my client had asked to see me. Because we had arranged it. He sent back and said, "No, he can't see me because he's not under arrest; he's a detainee and under detention orders and he's not entitled to a lawyer."

Under their laws, they could detain you for about sixty days and then they could renew it for another sixty days. The laws in Kenya were incredible. There were about seventeen things eventually that they could hang you for capital punishment for so many things. It's a terrible aberration of the law. And for several days, I kept the pressure up because I knew he wanted me and I knew the way he was, himself and the other leaders, Kamal, Achien Oneka, Kumerabi, Chairman Nichol, all the other leaders. All of them had been arrested. So I immediately sent wires by telephone. I telephoned the chief justice. I telephoned the chief of police.

I telephoned the governor, eventually, and sent a cable to the governor, who was Sir Edward Keeling. The governor whose appointment Jomo personally objected to. He was sent to Kenya only just a few months before Jomo was arrested. I sent a wire to him stating that in accordance with law, English law, a man is entitled to his defense; Kenyatta has asked for his defense and I have not been given any opportunity to see him. Will you rectify the situation? By that time, there was chaos in Kenya. The police were going around and beating up every Kikuyu they could find. The Riversend Market, which was called the Burma Market, was a large market covered with blood. They beat up every Kikuyu, even women and children. Everybody. They're being herded into dozens of trucks and sent off in carts and automobiles to detention centers. And I got back a very polite letter from the governor stating, he was very sorry that he delayed a letter but with the confusion taking place there, I would understand that matters were not as usual. I would be allowed to see Kenyatta but would not say where or when. He said he could not disclose the place where he would be for security reasons. But if I cared to come to Nairobi, a military plane would be put at my disposal and they would fly me to this undisclosed position. So I wrote back a letter stating that I flew in the last war. I flew for the Royal Air Force. But at least I knew when I flew who my enemies were.

Every day, we read in the newspapers here of people, of Kikuyu being missing, missing, missing believed killed. Am I going to allow myself to be added to that list by going to an undisclosed place? I said, "I'm sorry, I can't accept the position." But I demanded to see my client. There was no further reply. Nobody would tell me where he was. You couldn't find out. But we have an African plan working, an underground grapevine, one way or the other, one way or the other. One day, I used to go shooting every Saturday, hunting. When I was inside cleaning our guns, my house boy came to me and said, "Bwana, there's a white man outside that wants to see you." I said, "What does he want to see me about?" He said, "The matter is secret, private. He wants to speak to you privately." "Send him in." This huge man, whose name I am not entitled to disclose, I think his family is still living there. He was a government servant, had been in Kapengura. This was the first time I heard the name. And it is way up in the north, near to the Abyssinian border. He wanted me to go to Kapengura. That district up there. Nobody can go into that district unless you have a pass, a special pass. And the people there are particularly backward, practically naked. You see some of them completely naked. And they're very, very backward, no schools and post offices and that sort of thing.

Where the judge sat was an unused school, which had closed. There was no telephone or anything like that. So he couldn't get in touch with anybody. But this man was in court. They had to bring them into court and according to law, you can't try them while he's under detention. You have to release him from detention and then, when they're free, within five minutes or so, you can arrest him again, under ordinary criminal law. It still is the same law now. You can't try a man under detention. So this strange messenger was up there. He was a member of the press, working in the government department, information services. And when he was up there, he got a message. He said he was at a trial when they brought Jomo up for this release. And he brought me a message directly from Kenya. He said he had spoken to Kenyatta and Kenyatta had sent him to me to tell him where he was, and to come over there to Kapengura to defend him. They're going to try him next week Wednesday, which is only a few days away. His trial would go on then. And he said, "Tell him this," (because Jomo is a very wise man.) He told Jomo something which only Jomo and I would know, something that happened all the way in England. Only Jomo and I would know of that, to establish his credibility.

So when the man came and he discussed with me and said, well this, and he asked me to come over there to defend him, I said, well, you know, why should I trust you? How do I know this is not another trap? They had set several traps for me before. How do I know this is not another trap? He said, Jomo said to tell you, and he told me the secret, given to him by Jomo. Without a doubt, everything went all right. If that man knew that, Jomo would have sent that message to me. So I thanked him very much. He was tired. He had been driving for two days and two nights. Driving to come down there. So I sent a boy to get him shaved and bathed and breakfast and rest out quietly.

I promised that I would not disclose his name to anybody, to anybody. I next began to pack and I got in touch with my own district commissioner, who was a white South African, but a very liberal chap, a Rhodes Scholar himself. And I went to him and said that "I've got to go up there. I would like to get a pass. You are the district commissioner; you have the power, like a governor. Get me a pass." And he gave me a very generous pass, a pass to go on all roads, whatever, for Kenya, to the extent of the detention, as long as the detention order was on. So I had a generous pass all the time. I needed it tremendously, without which I couldn't move.

I started to pack my things, including my guns, my own guns, because I decided if this boy from Westmoreland is going to all these enemy areas, I am not just going alone. So I have them there and I drove in my car alone. And I drove and drove and drove to Nairobi, through, through two days. I was using a map. Some places just have an elephant trail. And I drove up there with about two days stubble of beard on myself, and my books.

And when I reached up there they stopped me at the Army post. I said, I've come to defend this man. I showed him my letter and pass. "Well, we will carry you to the courthouse. The trial at the courthouse is going to be today."

So they carried me in a Jeep. They went in front, a Jeep behind and a heli-
copter flying overhead. So after going through this, we drove into this place,
passed all sort of road blocks on the way to the prison, almost a semi-desert
country. And when I went up there, it was a very moving scene. I can hardly
describe the feeling when the men saw me. They heard my voice before they
saw me. By the way, the prisoner is practically under the ground, in a sort
of slit- like tank trap, sitting down, below ground level. I asked if I could
see my client? I didn't know where I could sit so I just heard a voice. But
they shouted my name and it was like "Jesus had come!" So there was I in
this courthouse, the only black man there, soldiers all over the place and the
prosecutor, a white Queen's Counsel, who was specially brought over from
England.

A Queen's Counsel is a title given to a celebrated barrister. He can be on
either side. It's a professional qualification. It's the highest qualification a
barrister can have, Queen's Counsel. And in Nigeria, they call them State
Advocates of Nigeria, SAN. But I went before this judge, and I can't think of
a worse judge than him, even the one in Bermuda who said his job was "to
reinforce the steel backbone of empire." This judge was a retired planter and
a real white redneck who had finished his time on the bench and retired. So
he had always been completely against anything African. He was specially
chosen and paid so much per day to look after this case.

It was a white stamp trial all over, which means it was a trial where everything was ready. It was really just a matter of carrying through the forms so
the world could see it. So there was I, alone up there. And the first thing the
judge asked me was, by what means did I come there? And I said "By what
means? I drove." And he said, "That's not what I mean. By what orders?
How do you?" He was trying to find out how did I know that the trial was
going to be there. It was not in the newspapers anywhere. I said, "I don't
think the question is relevant. But here are my qualifications that I brought."
I showed him my credentials. He said, "Well, I suppose you are who you say
you are." But I said "I have some preliminary motions to make." "What are
they," he said. Obviously tired of me before he started. I said, "I'm applying
for an adjournment." He said, "Impossible. Do you know what it has cost the
government to keep this man here? It's going to cost so much a day. Look
at the evidence we have." And I saw for the first time a bench full of books
and papers all over the court. I said, "You brought me here, you brought
the prisoner here, I didn't just come here. You brought me here and having
brought me here, I am entitled at least to know why you brought me here.
How do you know I am not going to plead guilty? I don't even know what
he is charged with. I don't even have a charge." So he thought for a minute,
then said, "Well, how much time do you need to read this?" And I said, "I

can't say, I can't say, because I don't know what the charges are. I'm going to apply for an adjournment for a matter of a few days." He said "Impossible." I said, "Well, I can't give you any other day until I see the charges." They gave me the charges, which was like a book. About fifty-odd pages on all five of the 5 accused.

When I had my meeting and talked to Jomo and the boys, just basically I'm talking to them, all in the cell, shackled. I didn't get through more than about two pages. I've been discussing things with Jomo and what is going to happen, what is happening, et cetera, explaining to him what the law was and what we're going to do with this. And then when the case was called up, the judge said, "Well, have you made up your mind now?" "Yes," I said, "I'm applying for an adjournment of two weeks." "Impossible! Impossible!" And then he started telling me what it was costing them. I said, "Well, I'm sorry, by your law, the law of Kenya, it will take ten days after you're inoculated to come into this country, to be allowed into the country. And this is a very important case. This is not just an ordinary case. It's a political case." At which they objected. "It's not a political; it is an ordinary criminal case." I said, "This is a political case, anyway I'm a very young lawyer, just qualified." I was 35 at that point. "I don't feel myself fit and up to the task of carrying on a case of this sort. I am applying overseas to get legal assistance to lead me in this matter, Queen's Counsel. He's entitled to Queen's Counsel as his opposition here. Jomo should have Queen's Counsel."

And the judge said, "Well, I don't see how I can give you that time." And the prosecutor said, "Well, My Lord, if I may, I have a word to say about this adjournment. I think he is entitled to a defense and if it takes ten days for counsel to come here, provided he starts today, two weeks is not a long burden." Because he agreed, the judge said, "All right, two weeks, and I'm going to go right on with the case."

I immediately dashed out of the court, went, and I said a few words to Jomo and the others. I couldn't send a cable from Kenya. I don't know where the other one is going to, don't know where the money is going to come from. I don't know who I'm going to get. I am on my own. I went out across the border from Kenya to Tanganyika, phoned a post office and sent out four cables: one cable to Norman W. Manley in Jamaica telling him, great African leader, et cetera, et cetera, Jomo Kenyatta is being tried, such-and-such. Would you kindly come and lead me at the defense? I sent another one to Sir Hartley Shaw Cross Q.C. who was attorney general for England and another to D.N. Pritt, who had just been elected the last socialist Q.C. Member of Parliament, a communist of East London. And one of the bravest lawyers I have ever seen and a good lawyer. And I forget to whom the fourth one was sent. I sent them off without knowing where the money was going to come from to pay them or what's going to happen. And I'm going to have to work through the immigration to get them into the country and all sorts of things, and I alone had to do it.

I went down to Nairobi to see if I could get any other lawyers. And none of the white lawyers there would even look at me. There was one black lawyer called Agwins Hodiak. He was married to an English woman and was working for the government. He said, no, no, no, no, he couldn't touch it. He couldn't touch it. I went to the great leaders around. I went to the leading Indian lawyer who was a Queen's Counsel but he refused too. No, he wasn't a Queen's Counsel then but he was a leading Indian criminal lawyer. And he said he had some pimples on his neck, and he was very sorry, he would love to. I could use his offices if I wanted. They were all dead scared. None would face the government. And I had to go back alone on my own.

One young Indian lawyer, Kapila-Achroo, no, a young Indian lawyer who said he would come and he would join. I didn't know the Kenya criminal code well either. I worked in the Tanganyika code and so on. And he came up with me in two weeks' time and the case started. The time had come soon. I arranged for a hotel accommodation for a Brit lawyer, Dingle Foote. There was an Indian man who was applying, the money would pay for his hotel, an Indian friend and client of mine. He had paid us, arranged for the hotel in his black book. And when we went to the hotel, when we went to the airport, I met him and brought him back to the hotel. But they wouldn't admit him because he was defending Kenyatta. All white, you know and we stayed with the same Indian man who was paying this, was going to pay for this. We became fast friends. I spoke to Kwame Nkrumah and said: "If you could send me some good African lawyers only to help us because this is obviously going to be a long case and I need a lot of help when they cross-examine the defendant and so on. I need a lot of workers." He said, OK, he'd send to us some. One came over, one came from Nigeria. H.O. Davis from Nigeria. Two from Kenya, five from India. I had also sent a wire to Nehru and Nehru sent five. He said one was a very, very learned, registrar of the Bengal Court, a man who proved very useful in his knowledge of the Indian Evidence Act, which is the act we used in Kenya. And four others.

But you know, Immigration wouldn't let them into Kenya. I went to the immigration officer but they seemed to think, you already have enough lawyers. You have "a gang of lawyers and you don't need a gang of lawyers. You don't need any more." And he wouldn't let them land. One had a diplomatic passport as he was an ex-ambassador to Turkey from the Indian bloc and he came on. And another one from Nigeria, these are the others, as Africans, they slipped in and they didn't notice that they were there. They came in on their own. So we only had about four, which you need about six, but the work was very divided.

Now the next thing was the accommodation. There was nowhere we could be accommodated as lawyers. We couldn't be put up anywhere. They were all white practitioners, everyone at the courthouse was. There was one little inn that was there and they would not admit black people in there, wouldn't have any Indians either. And we had to persuade Pritt, who was quite old; he would have been 65 or 70 at the time. Had to beg him to stay and beg him to stay and take charge of it there. And we would go back, backward and forward to Nairobi, every morning.

It would take four hours each way to drive back and forth. And we had to go down and in one incident the car turned over and Pritt got hurt. But it was tough going and in fact the woman whose taxi we hired, she was an African, they arrested her, put her in detention, too. It was hell.

But ultimately we had a trial that lasted fifty-eight trial days, including one break when they tried D.N. Pritt for contempt of court. That was a lovely, lovely trial. I've never seen anything so happy in a court. He had every confidence that they couldn't convict him. I know in Kenya, I didn't think anything beyond them at all. I was worried, worried stiff when he was cited for contempt of court. I said, "Man, we're in trouble. You're in contempt of court now. What's going to happen to us if you're in that bay?" He said, "Don't you mind, young fellow, don't you mind. They're not going to convict me. I've got a good lawyer." I said, "Who?" He said, "You." Have you ever seen a man looking for a hole to disappear into?

And he, of course, defended himself, you know. He had that sort of mind. He could look at a page and recall it almost word perfect. He was a fantastic lawyer. He had a good English judge from Jamaica at the Court of Appeals, who had known Manley and who had not been corrupted by the Kenyan environment or way of life. He wasn't one of the hardened lot. He tried the case, the contempt case. And so listening to the case, because they had to, they adjourned the principal case to a court so they would try the contempt charge. And people came from South Africa, all over West Africa, East Africa. Lawyers came to hear the trial of D.N. Pritt for contempt of court. Of course, we were looking for that. And after they heard on both sides, I remember the judge saying, "Excuse me, I'm going to adjourn this court for a moment while I write my judgment." Thousands of people came over to hear this case, this great white man who had been making such sharp repartees right through the case.[2] The Judge found D.N. Pritt not guilty of contempt.

At the case continued, the court not only found them guilty, including Kenyatta, but the judge said he believed all the witnesses for the prosecution and he disbelieved all the witnesses for the defense. It was a clear black and white decision. It went as far as this. The prosecution said, "I'm going to call a man, a priest, an African priest who is going to state that he was at an illegal oath-taking ceremony at a certain date at a certain place with some fifteen others where one of these illegal oaths were going to be, and were administered." This was one of the many charges against the men. I don't remember how many charges but that was one of them. And he was going to bring a priest who would prove that. Eventually when they'd finished their case without calling him as a witness, I said, "What about the priest you're bringing?" He said, "I couldn't find him."

Well, we found him. We found him and used him as a defense witness and he said exactly the opposite to what they expected. He knew nothing at all about it. He didn't know the case. He said he wasn't there and he showed his own diary that he was somewhere else on that day. It couldn't be he, he couldn't have been and he knew nothing at all about it. And none of the other people, of course, were there because the meeting didn't exist, something they fabricated. And the judge found, they disbelieved him. They disbelieved his diary and they believed the Crown. It was the biggest farce of a trial I have ever seen. And he sentenced them to five years' hard labor.

When Kenyatta was in prison, they extended his sentence to another two years, while he was in prison. And they took away his land and broke up his school. But they found out while he was there that things got worse outside. Well, after that, it was after that the Mau Mau thing started to break out in a big way because you know it was chiefly Africans being killed because they refused to join the oaths. Very few Europeans were killed; very, very few. The uprising had cost government a lot of money. They brought in the soldiers, a wing of the Royal Air Force. And the Mau Mau men fought as guerillas in a fantastic way. General China and some of the other fellows that were on the ground fought daily. They just couldn't find them, like shadows. And the people were terrorized. I know what terrorism means and I can give you the idea of how they were in terror of every black person they saw. They were in terror every day. When Kenyatta was found guilty, he made a great speech, which I think I still have somewhere. He made a speech. He forgave the judge. He says, you know, I know you have to do this and you had to do this and you do that because you belong to that group and that pack, et cetera, et cetera. But I'm speaking out to the world. All I'm asking for in my country and all I ever asked for is that they should be given a free education and they should be treated like human beings. A fine speech, saying exactly what he was asking for. And that none of the false charges against him should hold up.

I saw him after they took him away. I went up very early. Every year I went to see him. I went with their permission as his lawyer to go up to these places where they kept him in various places. In fact, I went there on medical grounds because at one stage his eyes were giving him trouble. Another time, his stomach was giving him trouble, according to the doctors there. And I tried to get lawyer Foote, Dingle Foote, to appeal for me to see if I could get them to move him. But he couldn't get in. And I used to see him, too. I have some pictures which I took of him in his prison garb. I don't think I have many of the legal papers. I believe I still have the actual trial notes. And I think I have a few photographs still. And the most I've ever had, you know, when I wrote that book, *From Kingston to Kenya*, I wrote it in its original and it was lost. The whole manuscript was lost. Dawes is a Jamaican from Ghana who was visiting with me. He was a good writer and he borrowed the manuscript to go out and edit it for me and he died and nobody knew what happened to my manuscript. It was three years of work. I started and I wrote back again this last one that you have there, which I have just recited to you.

Independence in Kenya

When Kenya obtained its independence, with Kenyatta as president, I was in Jamaica. They sent an invitation to me, the government sent one and then the Kenyatta family sent me another invitation asking me to come over to the Independence celebration. I had seen Kenyatta after he came out of prison, when he was there, when he was moving around. And I went around with him and he made some outstanding speeches showing the real man that he was. I remember him on his release going to a white settlement, a pure white area in the white highlands, where the farmers were, they were Klansmen, so to speak, and waiting there for him just to open his mouth. And they were all farmers, big white farmers, looking at him in the terms of which the governor had described him, "the Prince of Darkness and of Death," were the words the governor had used.

And I drove up with him. Jomo was there, he was very fond of me, and we drove up together, the president with his aides, his bodyguard and so on. And as he opened his mouth and spoke to them, the whole thing disappeared. I have never seen such a transformation. He began by saying, "We are all farmers, you and I, and all farmers want the same things for their family: good crops, good price, so that they can put clothes on their children and send them to the public schools. And all good farmers want it, whether you are white farmers or black." And he spoke to them in those terms. He could have them eating out of his hand by the time he finished. The whole Klansmen said, my God! This isn't the man we expected at all. And many there who had decided to leave the country stayed on because he was very, very generous to them, very generous. He had no revenge and his book, called *Suffering Without Bitterness*, shows this.

I always think that there are three men who had a similar character of forgiveness, all black. Jomo was one. Martin Luther King was another. And of course, Mandela is the arch- example of it all. Men who had been persecuted, men who had been wrongfully sent to prison for their people, and men who came out with forgiveness and without bitterness. I don't think any other race can equal that.

But I was really honored to be at the Independence celebration. The British have a set procedure which they always perform whenever they are having these independence ceremonies. They work up to it until the day and there's a big clock in the public stadium or wherever they're having it, the clock is ticking over and the crowd is there waiting in a tiptoe of expectancy, waiting for the hour to break when they are going to become free. And they always are jovial and everybody happy and laughing and drinking and generally enjoying it. And at midnight, the lights would lower and minutes after midnight, the lights would go on and you would see the new flag going up on one flagpole and on the other flagpole you'd see the Union Jack, the British flag, coming down at the same time.

The independence formula I have seen in Barbados, the Bahamas, Guyana, and Trinidad. I've seen that flag move all the way, and of course in my own Jamaica. But this in Kenya moved me more than most because of this huge stadium. There were lots of different ethnic groups there dancing in their own various costumes or lack of it. And they were all there dancing around and meeting. And I thought on the vast size of it. But I was sitting right up just behind Jomo. He was sitting beside the prince, I think Prince William. His white naval uniform, glistening with medals and ceremonial sword. Jomo was sitting in a European formal wear with a rose in his button hole. He carried his large elephant cane. There we were. The Prince and Jomo got up just before midnight. They left from their chairs and walked. And as they walked out there to take their posts each at his pole, I felt it. I really felt it because I remember a few months ago when that man was in a prison and he was walking inch by inch because of the shackles on his feet and the manacles on his hand and waist and is shuffling around, just to walk. Just a few months ago. Tonight striding out upon that stadium like a man, to take charge as President of his own country. It hit me. I tell you, that time it hit me. It really hit me. It impressed me more than the independence of my own country. Here's a man who fought for it and now he's on top, eventually. And he went out there and I saw that and that was just. And he never forgot it, you know. He never forgot. He never forgot me.

MATURATION OF PAN-AFRICAN THOUGHT

Thoughts on African Repatriation

My views on repatriation, I believe that all of the African countries should have, in their own constitution, "The right to return, all sons and descendants of people of African descent." They have every right to return, subject, of course, to any criminal record they may have. It should be one of their requests for reparations as part of the whole repayment for the slave trade. And I believe that it should be an organized matter. I think we both need each other. We in the West Indies and America know very little about Africa, very little.Very little indeed. It's a tremendous continent with deep history, deep, very deep and we should learn more about it and we should take the skills we learned with us over there.

I believe that one of the things we ask for is repatriation. Repatriation is that massive transfer of skills, that is thousands of people, West Indians, Africans, American blacks, training in the industries and the managerial level and otherwise, training in the industrial countries to go back to Africa to work. Massive, not two or three. Thousands. There should be exchanges of masses of people to bring them up to where they would have been if their history had not been interrupted by slavery. Because reparations is not repayment; it is repairing, to repair the damage that they did to our own development. And that damage has never been reimbursed yet, starting behind the eight ball the whole way. They've gone very far with their industries and with their universities, technology and things that we built for them out of our blood. So I think something like that, or, and including a Pan-African Marshall Plan. Those are some of the things we ask for in reparations. But as far as repatriation is concerned, if anybody wants to go back, they should go back but it should be organized. We don't want romantic types to go back, the romantic types who think they will go there to the land of milk and honey. Forget them. They're not contributing to anybody. But there should be an education process, a selective process and a two-way fare ticket. It should be organized by the governments or with well-known government organizations. There should be a preparation, otherwise there's going to be a culture shock.

But we have Stokely Carmichael, an African-American who, in the latter part of his career, went back to Africa and actually died there. And of course, Du Bois went back to Ghana.[3]

I think that warning is well said. I think America has used quite a few of her black men as ambassadors abroad, for obvious reasons, and all of them have not been in African interest. Because the things are so far apart, you know. The things are so far apart. Many Africans, many African-Americans who go there are disappointed in what they see because they don't know of

Africa and they see these shanties. They see the underdevelopment. They see the historical development has been broken, the nexus has been broken. We do not know African history and that's one of the first things we should be doing now. We should study, not just African history, but Pan-African history. Because when we think about African history in this country, we think about the liberationists, the Frederick Douglass's and the Harriet Tubmans and so on. But it goes much further than that. African-American history is not enough; we want Pan-African history. And I think that's a necessity; we'll study Pan-African history. Because you'll always come upon this long black hiatus where they said Africa had no history, because the Europeans believed that our history only began when there was a contact between Africans and Americans. Before that, "All was confusion." That is not true. We know where we are, we had an African history and we should study that.

Thoughts on Black Nationalism

I knew Walter Rodney and his book *How Europe Underdeveloped Africa* but was not close to him actually. I thought he was being useful in Tanzania or what he did at Jamaica, I said, for God's sake, he's a blessing to the country. In Tanzania they always watched him much too closely and I don't mean just the Europeans. I mean the Tanzanian government. They thought he was a little too far left. And he was a historian, you see, a great historian. And he fell into a little disfavor, not all too much, but he fell into a little disfavor.

I did not participate in the Sixth Pan-African Congress, but I went to the Seventh in Kampala, Uganda. And this last one, the last time I saw Stokely Carmichael. You know, "Black is Beautiful." You know who I'm talking about? Stokely Carmichael. Last time I saw Stokely Carmichael, he was there in the Seventh Pan-African Conference in Kampala.

NOTES

1. His brother died a few years ago.
2. The Dan Pritt case was resolved and then the Kenyatta case went on for fifty-eight days.
3. The Editor points out to the Ambassador that in his book, *Dark Days in Ghana,* Nkrumah makes reference to Franklin Williams, an African-American, who apparently was the United States Ambassador to Ghana at the time he was deposed. And Nkrumah said that Africa had to be careful about African-Americans who came there under the guise of helping but in reality were working to undermine Ghana's political and economic independence. Ambassador Thompson had a clear response to Nkrumah's warnings.

Bill Sutherland[1]

EARLY LIFE AND DEVELOPMENT

I was born in Lynchburgh, New Jersey. Actually, I was born in Orange, New Jersey and then when I was six months old my family moved to Glenridge, New Jersey. You know, these are the suburban towns. I stayed there during most of my schooling up to high school. Then I attended Bates College in Maine. I graduated in 1940. And after that I traveled a bit because I was working for the Student Peace Service of the Friends. They had projects in Chicago. That was simply a summer volunteer effort and after that I was with David Dellinger and a group in Newark, New Jersey. We had what we called then Ashram. It was based upon the Indian Gandhian approach. We worked in what I'd call a blighted area. It was not a slum but it was a down-at-the-heels area of Newark, primarily African-American. When we had a cooperative, we worked with children. We worked out of a church.

Opposition to War

In the meantime I also was the Secretary of the Youth Committee Against War in New York. So I combined those two jobs until 1942 when I refused to go into the Civilian Public Service Camp. And that's when I was convicted and sentenced to four years in prison.

You know people took different positions on the draft. Dellinger and some of the others were non-registrants. Others stopped at resistance. Others stopped at physical. My position was that I would do all of those things, but at the time the government put me away when I was doing my anti-war work, that was when I would take my stand. So, I refused to go Civilian Public Service Camp and spend the war in the woods. That was the charge.

45

One basis of my position against the war was this. If I believed that war was a way to stop fascism, I would not go to Germany. I would go to Alabama, or Georgia or Mississippi, if that was the way. But I had already, even from my high school days had already become influenced by the non-violent revolutionary approach. And so that was one basis. The other at that time was fairly conventional Christian pacifism. Which I have to say I no longer take that position in such a conventional way.

I spent thirty-eight months in prison actually with the good-time system. We were really on strike a number of times within the prison system against racial segregation, against censorship and so on. At the time that I was released at thirty-eight months we were actually carrying on an action but the prison system was so glad to get rid of us that at the end of the war, they just tossed us out. David Dellinger was convicted twice. They played the cat and the mouse game on him. And the first time he spent time in Danbury, Connecticut on a year-and-a-day basis and then the second time he came to where I was, which was Lewisburg, Pennsylvania, a medium-custody prison, and he joined us in our strike against segregation in the prison system.

It was a federal penitentiary at the same time we are segregated. It was an honorable profession. This was just a risk of the game. And many of these people who were black and white had to work very closely with the whites making the whiskey and the blacks being the runners. And very often the Blacks would go up and stay with the whites and then hit the road in the morning. But when they came into the prison system they were segregated.

My parents were very upset by me being in prison because my father was a dentist. I guess a Buppie in today's parlance. He and my mother were both very unhappy because they had pictured me going to law school in Michigan and so on. However, I think that they became somewhat reconciled to it when a number of my classmates, particularly a man name Frank Coffin who became a federal judge, went into the Navy and wrote my parents and said, "Well, you know, this is a time when people have to make a choice. We respect Bill's choice." The friends and family gradually came to understand. You know they were not happy at all with my position.

PAN-AFRICAN CONSCIOUSNESS AND ACTIVISM

Development of Interest in Africa

After I came out of the prison I developed an interest in Africa. This is an interesting thing. In my family's history we have what I call "Roots Without Sweat." Because on my father's side there was an old patriarch. Incidentally, I should say that this whole story is called "A Tale of Two

Continents." And it's in the February 1975 issue of *Ebony.* Eva Bell Thompson is the author of this. It has Barbara Jordan on the cover. And in it there's this story of this patriarch, Scipio Vaughan, who was a slave, who had a master in Virginia, I think. And he was a skilled carpenter. His master was a sort of humane man and said, "Look, I'm dying of tuberculosis. If you will use the proceeds of your skill to educate my children, I will free you." So he freed him and Scipio married a Cherokee woman and they had thirteen children. And on his deathbed he told his two eldest sons, "Look, I was born in Abeokuta, Nigeria. I want you to leave this land of oppression and go back home." So, the two sons went back to Abeokuta, but they kept in touch with the family in the states. And so, when I was very young my father would take me to see cousin Aida in New York, who had come from Africa. It didn't mean anything to me. She gave me a brightly colored palm fan. I didn't think much of it at the time. So that's one aspect of my African connection. And incidentally, I have gone to Africa. I have seen the grave of one of the sons. It says on it: "His father told him to leave the land of oppression."

But the real consciousness came in 1951. And in 1951 Dellinger, Ralph Diga, and I and Arthur Emory were engaged in a project in opposing the Iron Curtain and the Cold War. But we started off. The idea was to cycle from Paris to Moscow, taking this message. But in Paris I met many Africans. The message was let us ignore the Iron Curtain. And we were war objectors who refused to fight in our own country. We went to the Russian soldiers and allied soldiers with these leftists calling on them to refuse to fight. Sort of crazy, but that's a whole other story, which is too long and I don't want to get into it.

In essence, we started in Paris and I met African students there who were committed to fighting for the liberation of their countries. And when the project was over I was asked to go to England to speak about it and that was where I met George Padmore and other Pan-Africanists and some more students, so the other key thing was I spoke about the project at the Selly Oaks Colleges. Those are Quaker colleges in Birmingham, England. That time I met a South African editor of *The Bantu World.* And he told me that there was going to be this great campaign called the Defiance Against Unjust Laws in South Africa in 1952. And he gave me all the names. So when I went back to the United States I got in touch with Bayard Rustin and George Houser and we started Americans for South African Resistance, which later became American Committee on Africa. But I had wanted to go myself to Africa and the movement had been very much against it. They said we need you at home. But in the meantime Rustin had arranged for me to get to Africa. And as a matter of fact he was due to go to Nigeria to work with Azikiwe. And unfortunately for Bayard he got arrested on a homosexual charge and we discussed it and I was to take his place. Well, I never got to Nigeria at that time because obviously there was some connection between the MIS and the CIA and they must have had a dossier on me. The Colonial Office kept me sort of hanging for months in England, but finally we were able to swing another deal because the Gold Coast, this is 1953, had obtained what they called Internal Self Government which meant that although they did not have charge of defense or finances or foreign affairs, they had charge of immigration. So George Padmore and a British MP in the Movement for Colonial Freedom, named Reginald Sorenson, wrote letters to Kwame Nkrumah. He and along with Fenner Brockway were men who were members of Parliament who were for freedom in India and freedom in Africa and so on. So they had these connections with Nkrumah along with Padmore. So they wrote and recommended that I get my visa for the Gold Coast and I got it that way. Incidentally, the letters were taken by Arthur E. Morgan. He was a Quaker. He, at one point was head of Antioch College. At that time he was head of TVA, Tennessee Valley Authority. So the British had called upon him to advise them, so we did an end-around run of the Colonial Office. And we gave the letters to Morgan and he took them to Nkrumah. That's how I got there. That was at the end of '53. December of '53. I was kept in England from May to December. Waiting to get the chance to go.

I met Padmore in 1951. He must have been about 50 and I was in early 30s. I always called him the Thomas Paine of the Pan-African Movement because he was the pamphleteer and the theoretician. He had not written his book, *Pan-Africanism or Communism* at the time I met him. I think it came out a couple of years later. But I didn't know too much about that at the time. But Padmore was really the Doyen and he had great discussions in his kitchen with his wife, Dorothy, serving the food and so on. Then later on of course he became a very close advisor to Nkrumah. In fact, he had been an advisor before, but he became formally an advisor to him when Ghana became independent.

Before I went to the Gold Coast in September '53 I had not come into contact with any of the Pan-African leaders of the early Pan-African Congresses. Except I had been a neighbor in the late 40s, neighbor, '47, '48 of C.L.R. James because we both lived in the East Village and I learned a great deal from C.L.R and we remained close friends all during the period and the Gold Coast and when it became Ghana and then Tanzania. We were periodically together. He was a real major influence, I think, on my life. W.E.B. Du Bois and I had only met at parties and had no chance for a discussion with him the way I had with C.L.R.

Pan-African Influence

I think really James had more influence on my thinking than Padmore. Simply because he was a person with whom I had much closer friendship, personal relationship with. Padmore used to shake his head about me because he came out of the Marxist tradition and I had this idea about the West had made its major contribution in terms of science and technology and the external world. And the East had made its major contribution in the internal world and the spiritual world. But that in terms of giving things life and warmth that Africa could make its contribution there. And for Padmore, that was a lot of nonsense. But a Pan-Africanist of any kind he was in favor of. But it would have been more the thing that Archbishop Tutu talks about in terms of the Ubuntu Concept. I just had my own undeveloped thoughts along those lines.

By 1953, I was evolving into something else because in prison I had seen so much of what was violence but was not physical violence, that I came out of prison thinking that as long as you don't kill em, it was alright. But I think what had happened to me was that I was still firmly committed of the Gandhian concept of non-violence and it was in that direction that I was leaning. Anarchist. I don't want to say anarchist because I don't think I could be given a card-carrying thing. But certainly a great belief in the action of people in small group activities. I was influenced by A.J. Muste. He was known as the number one pacifist in the radical pacifist circles. But he was a person who had been a Presbyterian minister and then became very much involved in the labor movement, but then after that for a while he was involved with the Trotskyists, then he came back and came into this Gandhian approach. So, I think that I'm sort of a maverick and it's hard for me to place myself outside of these two mainstreams, Pan-Africanism and Gandhian approach.

By '53, I was very enthusiastic at the Pan-African level but I still carried on the belief. As a matter of fact in that period this was a time when there was a great enthusiasm for the Gandhian approach because India had just been freed. Now Padmore was a very pragmatic man and he thought that, well, since India was able to do it, maybe this was a way for Africa. And you know Nkrumah himself used what he called positive action. That was a major thing. With Kenneth Kaunda, he was a Gandhian on principle. He later turned after he became President of Zambia. And Nyerere was a very pragmatic non-violent person. Not a pacifist by any means. So that was very much in the air on the one hand, and then on the other there was Algeria. And Fanon and the people who felt that armed struggle was necessary.

My guess was that the Algerian Revolution had started by 1956. But Fanon came to Ghana in early 1960 as the representative of the FLN in Ghana. But we had a number of conversations. It was very interesting and we discussed this thing. He said we tried this non-violence, but then the French would go into the Casbah and they would knock on a door and take out the head of the household and shoot him in the middle of the street. And when they did that thirty-five or forty times then the whole idea of non-violent resistance went down the drain. But you see, the way that Fanon has been touted as the great advocate of violence does a great deal of injustice to him. He felt it was necessary for people to free themselves of this slave mentality by struggle, but there was a positive action conference in 1960. In 1959 the French had decided to use the Sahara as a testing ground for nuclear devices and we had a big campaign. We all were going into the Sahara Desert to put our bodies in the way of their efforts. Anyway, when the French did explode that device and simultaneously Sharpeville Massacre took place, Nkrumah called this conference in March, April, 1960. Fanon was there and it was so interesting because of all the people who spoke, he was the one who was the least romantic about armed struggle. He thought it was necessary. He was a man who had seen what war could do. He was not a person who glorified violence. He was a person who was not that in any sense.

Work in the Gold Coast

I remained in the Gold Coast from 1953 to 1957. And I was headmaster of a little secondary school in the Eastern region of the Gold Coast. But in 1957 Dr. Marguerite Cartwright, an African-American, contacted me. She was one of the early brilliant black women who had been in the Chorus Line of the Cotton Club, but then became a scholar and academic. Marguerite knew the Minister of Finance, Gbedema. He was one of the big three, along with he and Nkrumah and a man named Botsio. They were the big three of the Convention People's Party. Marguerite said this man needs someone to work with him and she was going to knock their heads together, so I became the private secretary of Gbedema. The point is that once I became private secretary I was in the States all the time. Because there would be the World Bank meetings and there would be a Commonwealth meeting in Canada or something like that. So that in fact maybe this would be of interest. Gbedema came over in 1958 and I was with him.

And we were taken by some African-American professors to a college in Delaware and on the way back we stopped at this Howard Johnsons. These professors said, you know, Mr. Gbedema, you can get something to eat in New Jersey, but here this is Route 40, you can't. Gbedema said "I don't believe it. Let's stop and let me go into this place." And so I knew what was going to happen, but I wasn't going to be the person to wash the dirty linen of the United States Government, so I went in with him and he was refused. When we came back from Delaware to New York, the press got a hold of the story and the next thing I know there was a call from the White House. And this was when Eisenhower was in power. And Eisenhower's token black at that time was a man name E. Frederic Morrow. Fred used to go around with my eldest sister so Fred said the president wants to invite your Minister for breakfast because he has been through so and so. We had a huge debate about this because if Eisenhower had took on everybody who had been discriminated against he had to open up a chain of Howard Johnsons himself. However, it was decided that if the president wanted us we would go. And I didn't get to go to that dinner. Fred Morrow just took me aside, but the point is this: that was the beginning of a real change on Route 40, in terms of discrimination.

I had decided in 1953 that I was leaving the States. That was a time at the height of the McCarthy period. I was totally in error about the resilience of movements because I didn't foresee the Civil Rights Movement or the anti-Vietnam movement. I thought people were knuckling under. My mother and father had died and I had decided that I would throw in my lots with the liberation movements of Africa.

NOTES

1. This interview was recorded on November 15, 2000 at the Annual Meeting of the African Studies Association, held in Nashville, Tennessee. Bill Sutherland was on a very tight schedule on that day and so the Editor was unable to obtain an extensive interview

Conclusions

After the 1945 Pan-African Congress in Manchester, England, the African involvements of Thompson and Sutherland took different paths. Coming from a colonial context, Ambassador Thompson had to overcome legally enforced racism in Jamaica to become a successful Air Force pilot and barrister. Bill Sutherland, from a privileged economic background, rejected material comfort and the use of violence as a tool for resolving international conflicts. Prior to the Congress, Bill Sutherland had refused to participate in America's war industry during World War II and, as a result, received a felony conviction and prison time. Ambassador Thompson, on the other hand, joined in Britain's fight against Hitler's Germany despite the racial marginalization that characterized his country, Jamaica. In both cases, these men possessed extraordinary personal traits of courage and tenacity.

Despite their differences over World War II, both men developed firm views on African self-help. Both recognized that they were descendants of Africa and therefore had a responsibility to the continent. Both recognized that, though separated by thousands of miles of oceans and land, they, as African people, had to "link up their struggles," as Professor Tony Martin has urged.

Much of this linkage grew out of the Pan-African movements that developed during the first half of the twentieth century. These movements of African self-help and unity were forged by men and women of the African diaspora, most notably through organizations like the African Association in London, founded in 1897.

Furthermore, it is no coincidence that a barrister from the African diasporic community of Trinidad, Henry Sylvester Williams, launched the London fraternal organization in 1897 and the first Pan-African Congress in 1900. Like Ambassador Thompson, Sylvester Williams was trained in the

European rule of law and both understood the inherent contradictions in a European jurisprudence that espoused grand ideals of justice and equality yet deprived African people the world over of political independence and human equality. Therefore upon finishing his legal studies as a barrister in London, Ambassador Thompson set out for Africa to perfect these legal ideals among the struggling masses of East Africa. Consequently, as a young lawyer he provided legal assistance to the most important African freedom movement in East Africa, the Mau Mau Rebellion. He represented the leader of this freedom movement, Jomo Kenyatta, and helped President Julius Nyerere of Tanzania lay the foundation for a unique African independent nation that was rooted in African communal concepts. Few young lawyers from the African diaspora have contributed so much at such an early point in their careers to African political and legal development as did Ambassador Dudley Thompson.

Bill Sutherland's ideological purity, manifested through an outright rejection of war and capitalist forms of exploitation, laid an important blueprint for Pan-African activists. His work recognized that war is generally the first response of nations when the control of massive capitalist wealth is lodged in an elite ruling class. His rejection of capitalism and violence mirrored the non-western ideological tenets of Gandhi and foreshadowed the later non-violent Civil Rights Movement in the American South. More importantly, Bill Sutherland embraced the economic concept of socialism at a time when the United States engaged in a widespread witch hunt to expose and punish anyone who dared embrace an economic paradigm other than monopoly capitalism. We must, therefore, credit Bill Sutherland for standing up for his beliefs in the face of such overwhelming opposition from American political and economic hegemony.

Finally, both men made their way to Africa where they found a welcome place to work for African advancement. Though on different coasts of the vast continent, they applied their considerable skills to the efforts of nation building.

Their efforts should serve as an inspiration to the children of the African diaspora in the twenty-first century as well. Ambassador Thompson has eloquently spoken of the need for reparations and limited repatriation efforts. He argues that Africa is in need of skilled labor, and such help should come from the African diaspora. Both men argue that the AIDS epidemic is a crisis that should draw attention and support from all quarters of the African diaspora and from others who recognize the crisis as a worldwide threat.

Finally, the lessons to be learned from the experiences of these two Pan-African activists are clear. Once African people the world over understand their connection to the continent of Africa, they must lend "Mother Africa" support. Yet this support will not be in the form and manner required or allowed by the western powers that have a racist and economic agenda for the continent. African people must chart their own path, realizing that the interests of Africa and western nations have been at odds over the past four hundred years. Only African unity around a progressive and mutually beneficial agenda will lead the continent to a more egalitarian and secure future.

Bibliography

Angelou, Maya, *All God's Children Need Travelin' Shoes* (New York: Vintage/Random House, 1987).

Baldwin, James, *The Fire Next Time* (New York: Laurel, 1964).

Bastide, Roger, *African Civilization in the New World* (New York: Harper and Row, 1971).

Crisis, "The Pan-African Congresses: The Story of a Growing Movement," October 1927.

Cronon, E. D., *Black Moses* (Madison: University of Wisconsin Press, 1955).

Counter, S. Allen, and David Evans, *I Sought My Brother* (Cambridge: MIT Press, 1981).

Campbell, Horace, *Rasta and Resistance: From Marcus Garvey to Walter Rodney* (Trenton: Africa World Press, 1987).

Du Bois, W.E.B., *The Autobiography of W.E.B. Du Bois* (New York: New World Publishers, 1968).

Davison, R.B., *Black British: Immigrant to England* (London: Oxford University Press, 1966).

Davidson, Basil, *The Liberation of Guinea* (Baltimore: Penguin Books, 1969).

Esedebe, Olisauwuche, *Pan-Africanism: The Idea and the Movement, 1776 to 1963* (Washington, D.C.: Howard University Press, 1982).

Fanon, Frantz, *Toward the African Revolution* (New York: Grove Press, 1967).

Harris, Sheldon H., *Paul Cuffe: Black America and the African Return* (New York: Simon and Schuster, 1972).

Johnson, Jr., Robert, *Why Blacks Left America for Africa: Interviews with Black Expatriates, 1971- 1999* (New York: Praeger, 2000).

Kenyatta, Jomo, *Facing Mt. Kenya* (New York: Vintage, 1962).

Kilson, Martin, *Political Change in a West African State* (Sierra Leone) (Cambridge: Harvard University Press, 1966).

Kodjoe, Ofuatey, *Pan-Africanism: New Directions in Strategy* (Lanham: University Press of America, 1986).

Jenkins, David, *Black Zion: Africa Imagined and Real, As Seen by Today's Blacks* (New York: Harcourt Brace Jovanovich, 1975).

Legume, C., *Pan Africanism* (New York: Praeger, 1965).

Lotchie, M., *Zanzibar: Background to Revolution* (Princeton: Princeton University Press, 1965).

Markovitz, I., *Leopold Senghor and the Politics of Negritude* (New York: Atheneum, 1969).

Marable, Manning, *African and Caribbean Politics: From Kwame Nkrumah to Maurice Bishop* (London: Verso, 1987).

Martin, Tony, *The Pan-African Connection: From Slavery to Garvey and Beyond* (Dover: The Majority Press,1985).

——, *Race First* "The Ideological and Organizational Struggles of Marcus Garvey and the Universal Negro Improvement Association" (Dover: The Majority Press, 1986)

Morgenthau, Ruth S., *Political Parties in French Speaking West Africa* (London: Clarendon Press, l964).

Mphahlele, E., *The African Image* (New York: Prager, 1962).

Nkrumah, Kwame, *Handbook of Revolutionary Warfare: A Guide to the Armed Phase of the African Revolution* (New York: International Publishers, 1969).

——, *Neo-Colonialism: The Last Stage of Imperialism* (London: Heinemann Educational Books, 1970).

——, *Dark Days in Ghana* (New York: International Publishers, 1968).

——, *Handbook of Revolutionary Warfare* (New York: International Publishers, 1969).

Nyerere, Julius, *Freedom and Socialism* (Oxford: Oxford University Press, 1968).

——, *Ujamaa: Essays on Socialism* (Oxford: Oxford University Press, 1968).

Hiro, Dilip, *Black British, White British* (London: Eyre and Spottiswoode, 1971).

Olisanwuche, Esedebe P., *Pan-Africanism: The Idea and Movement, 1776 to 1991*, Second Edition, (Washington, D.C., Howard University Press, 1994).

Odinga, Oginga, *Not Yet Uhuru* (New York: Hill and Wang, 1967).

Okello, John, *Revolution in Zanzibar* (Nairobi: East African Publishing House, 1965).

Quaison-Sackey, Alex, *Africa Unbound* (New York: Praeger, 1962).

Republic of Kenya, *African Socialism* (Sessional Paper No. 10 of 1963/5 (Nairobi: Government Printer, 1966).

Rosberg, C., W. Friedland (eds.), *African Socialism* (Stamford: Hoover Institute, 1965).

Rodney, Walter, *How Europe Underdeveloped Africa* (Washington, D.C.: Howard University Press, 1980).

Scobie, Edward, *Black Britannia: A History of Blacks in Britain* (Chicago: Johnson Publishing Company, 1972).

Senghor, Leopold, *On African Socialism* (New York: Praeger, 1964).

Sutherland, Bill; Meyer, Matt, *Guns and Gandhi in Africa: Pan-African Insights on Nonviolence, Armed Struggle, and Liberation* (Trenton, Africa World Press, 2000).

Thompson, Vincent Bakpetu, *Africa and Unity: The Evolution of Pan-Africanism* (London: Longway, 1969).

Winch, Julie, *Philadelphia's Black Elite,* "Activism, Accommodation, and the Struggle for Autonomy, 1787 to 1848" (Philadelphia: Temple University Press, 1988).

Wallerstein, Immanuel, *Africa: The Politics of Independence* (New York: Random House, 1961).

Walters, Ronald W., *Pan-Africanism in the African Diaspora* (Detroit: Wayne State University Press, 1997).

Welch, C., *Pan Africanism: Dream of Unity* (Ithaca: Cornell University Press, 1967).

Williams, Eric, *Capitalism and Slavery* (New York: Capricorn, 1966).

Index

www.ingramcontent.com/pod-product-compliance
Lightning Source LLC
Chambersburg PA
CBHW021824270326
41932CB00007B/323